MW01587512

Making Effective Presentations Pocket Tips Booklet
A tactical tool for developing and delivering effective presentations.

Designed and written by Barry J. McLoughlin.

For information, contact Barry McLoughlin Associates Inc.:
In the U.S.A. -
1825 Eye Street NW, Suite 400, Washington, D.C. 20006.
In Canada -
55 Metcalfe Street, Suite 1030, Ottawa, Ontario K1P 6L5.
Web Site: www.mclomedia.com
Email: communicate@mclomedia.com

To place an order please see the Appendix Tab at the end of this booklet.

Published by: McLoughlin MultiMedia Publishing Ltd.

Washington, D.C.	Princeton, N.J.	Ottawa, Canada
202-429-5243	609-951-2204	613-230-9235

In North America call toll free: 1-800-663-3899

Table of Contents

Table of Contents

Committees and Meetings

Audience Questions

Winning Debates

Appendix

Introduction

Foreword

Welcome to the Making *Effective Presentations* Pocket Tips Booklet. This booklet has been designed to help you communicate with greater skill and confidence in speeches, presentations, committee appearances, debates and more.

As a child in Ireland, my attempts to communicate were complicated by a stammer. The more I wanted to say, and the more excited I was, the more pronounced my stammer became. Later on in school, I recall the agonies I would endure in the weeks leading up to a class presentation or speech. By the time I entered high school, I became determined to overcome these challenges and essentially taught myself to confront my greatest fears. This Pocket Tips Booklet is a chance to share with you what I have learned and practiced (and am still learning and practicing) in public speaking, presentations, seminars and media interviews.

The launch of this brand new Making Effective Presentations Pocket Tips Booklet coincides with the release of the all-new Communicate with Power® Gold Box set of pocket tips booklets. The Gold Box Set includes *Making Effective Presentations*, *Risk and Crisis Communications* and the *Encountering the Media*® Pocket Tips Booklets. These products have been developed as easily accessible, concise planning tools for busy people.

This book is dedicated to my father 'J.R.' whose character and communications skills have always been the object of my admiration.

Barry McLoughlin
May, 1996

McLoughlin MultiMedia Publishing Ltd.

The Principals

Barry J. McLoughlin, president, founded Barry McLoughlin Associates Inc. in 1984, following a career as a television writer, interviewer and producer. Barry is a media trainer, communications consultant and media commentator. He designed and authored the training programs and tools published by McLoughlin MultiMedia Publishing Ltd.

Barry received his Master of Public Administration Degree from Harvard University (1983).

Laura M. Peck, vice-president of Barry McLoughlin Associates Inc. since 1984, is a former broadcaster and teacher. A graduate of Dalhousie University (Bachelor of Arts 1977, Bachelor of Education 1978), Laura is responsible for conducting seminars in presentation skills and media communications. She has coached political candidates and Fortune 500 CEOs in media and presentation skills.

Barry McLoughlin Associates Inc.

Barry McLoughlin Associates Inc. was founded in 1984 and has developed an international reputation for quality communications skills training programs. The firm has assembled a team of seminar leaders, trained in the copyrighted communications techniques of the company. Barry McLoughlin Associates Inc. conducts seminars for major corporations, government agencies, national associations and labor unions throughout North America and through licensed distributors around the world.

All of the seminars are customized, skills-oriented, training programs conducted on an in-house, small group basis.

McLoughlin MultiMedia Publishing Ltd.

McLoughlin MultiMedia Publishing Ltd. is a subsidiary of Barry McLoughlin Associates Inc., and produces state-of-the-art communications tools.

The product line includes the Encountering the Media® video and software program as well as the Communicate With Power™ Gold Box Set of pocket tips booklets.

For more information on products and seminars, please turn to the Appendix.

Introduction

With enormous changes sweeping every industry, government and non-profit organization today, the ability to present clear thoughts in a persuasive manner has never been more highly valued. A presentation is where you can make or break a sale, a job interview, a vitally important presentation to shareholders, board of directors, legislative committees, or to millions of people on television. No wonder that a *Fortune Magazine* survey revealed years ago that public speaking was rated as the number one fear of executives - even over dying!

This Making Effective Presentations Pocket Tips Booklet will help you plan and prepare many different kinds of presentations as well as deliver them effectively. It covers major formal speeches and informal presentations, debates, sales demonstrations, making introductions and even toasts.

What are 'Presentations'?

All of us present ideas, every time we open our mouths. We even present ourselves with purely non-verbal communications - our body language. Whether we stop for a brief hallway conversation, stand up and make a formal speech or engage in a meeting, we are presenting ourselves to others - who we are, what we believe and how we think of ourselves, our colleagues, clients, constituents and others.

5-Stage Process

By the time you have been introduced for your speech,
presentation or debate, many hours will (or should) have
gone into the event. Ninety percent of the success of a
speech or presentation lies below the surface - in planning
and preparing.

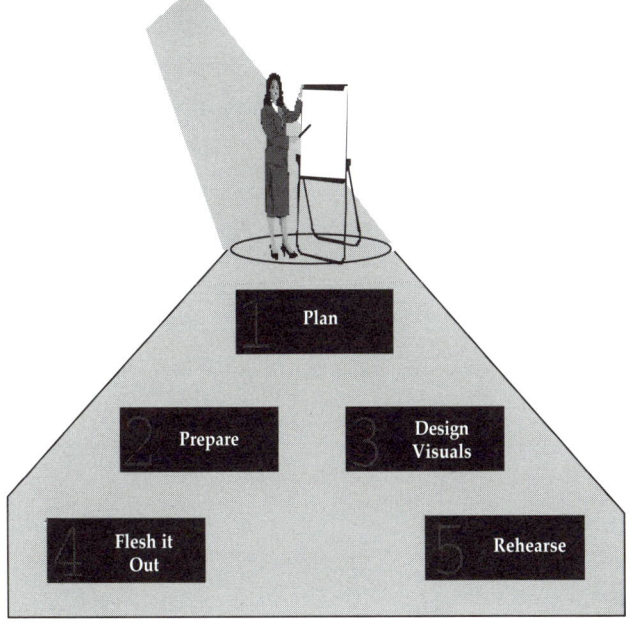

1 Plan

- *analyze your audience*
- *establish your goals*
- *define your messages*

Analyze Your Audience

Determine

- What is the preconceived audience attitude towards your subject: positive, negative, neutral, unknowing, uncaring?
- What are some possible concerns because of the audience's attitude?
- Where should the emphasis of your presentation be focused?
- Why should your audience care about your subject or message?

How to Find Out About Your Audience?

Sources
- event organizer
- audience members - arrange for a talk with a sample group or send a questionnaire in advance
- speakers who have previously addressed the group
- literature from sponsoring organization
- subject area specialists

The wider you cast your net the greater understanding you will gain about your audience.

Planning Tools

The following tools outline various approaches for analyzing your audiences and identifying your goals.

The Link Between Audience and Goals - The Communicate With Power Persuasion Ladder™

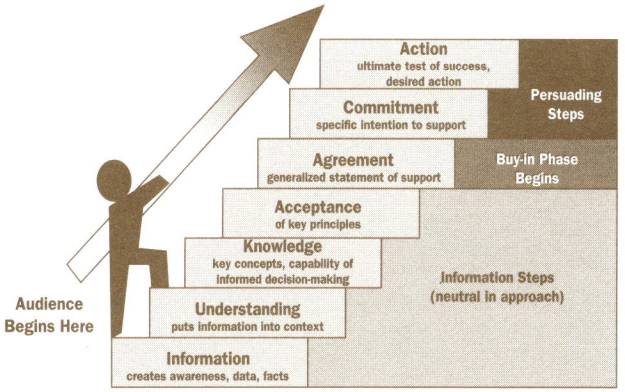

Ask:
　　At what step is the audience now, and how much
　　further up can I move them?

Do not try to over-reach when you set the goals for your presentation. Limit your goals and focus on accomplishing them.

Establish Your Goals

- Focus your goals on those who are open to your message.
- Counter strong critics credibly so that their views do not gain momentum with those who are open to persuasion.
- Your goals might include shifting soft critics to neutral, neutral audiences to soft supporters.
- With strong supporters, your goal is not to persuade but to reinforce or maintain their support while broadening your base with those who are open to your message.

Communicate With Power Goal Determinator™

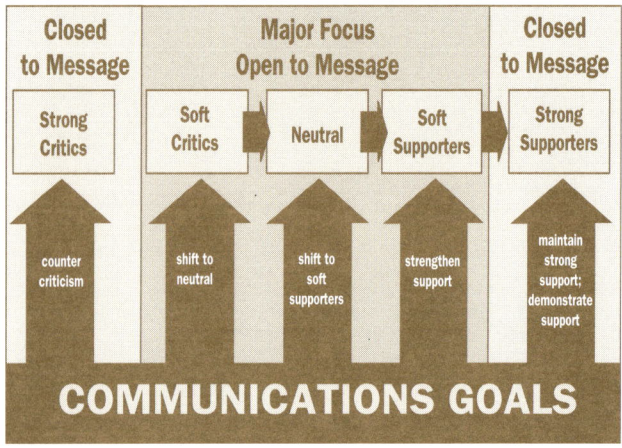

Consider the Audience's Perspective

Know who your audience is, why you were invited and what you want the audience to know, think, feel or be able to do as a result of your presentation or speech.

Set your objectives from the audience's perspective. When your presentation is over, the audience will:

- **know**... not an information 'dump' but an enhanced knowledge level, better able to make informed decisions
- **think**... about your topic, your message
- **feel**... perceptions about you, your team, your party, your competence
- **be able to do**... tangible actions

Communicate With Power Audience Planner™

Audience:

Why this audience?

What can the audience do with this information?

What is the preconceived audience attitude:
Positive ❒   Negative ❒   Unknowing ❒   Uncaring ❒

At what step is the audience?
Information ❒   Understanding ❒   Knowledge ❒
Acceptance ❒   Agreement ❒   Commitment ❒
Action ❒

Audience Analysis	My Goal
❒ Strong Critics	❒ Counter/Neutralize Critics
❒ Soft Critics	❒ Shift to Neutral
❒ Neutral	❒ Shift to Soft Supporters
❒ Soft Supporters	❒ Strengthen Support
❒ Strong Supporters	❒ Maintain Support

What do you want the audience to...

Know ————————————————————

Think ————————————————————

Feel ————————————————————

Be able to do ————————————————

Define Your Messages

What is a message?

A message is a succinct statement that captures the essence of your point. Rarely more than one or two sentences, a message must be easy to understand and retain. Ask yourself: "what do I want the audience to think about long after my presentation is over?"

The Core Message...

The overall, or core message, is your focus point and will form the focus point or the heart of your speech. Aim your speech towards the focus point, and your core message will drive the speech from start to finish.

Specific Messages...

Specific messages tell the audience how to achieve the overall message.

Enabling or Support Message

What the audience must know is order to understand or accept the specific messages. Each specific message might contain up to three enabling or support messages.

Establish Your Theme

The word or phrase which captures the values, vision or goals of the subject (freedom, dignity, family, leadership, vision, competition, against all odds, making a difference, etc.).

Sample:

Success for our organization means developing a whole new vision.	**Overall Message**
That means 1) tighter control over spending, 2) a sharper market focus and 3) a productive work force.	**3 Specific Messages**
Tighter control over spending is necessary because our costs have risen twice as quickly as our revenues.	**Enabling or Support Message**
A new vision.	**Theme**

The Communicate With Power Structure™
Overall Message:
Specific Message 1:
Enabling or Support Messages: 1. ———————————————————— 2. ———————————————————— 3. ————————————————————
Specific Message 2:
Enabling or Support Messages: 1. ———————————————————— 2. ———————————————————— 3. ————————————————————
Specific Message 3:
Enabling or Support Messages: 1. ———————————————————— 2. ———————————————————— 3. ————————————————————

The Communicate With Power Message Developer™

(For more detail, please see the Encountering the Media® Pocket Tips Booklet.)

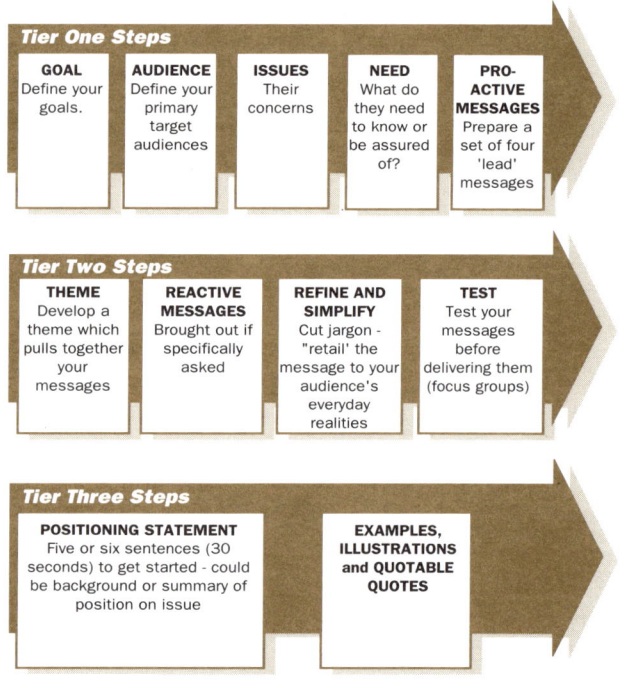

Tier One Steps

GOAL	AUDIENCE	ISSUES	NEED	PRO-ACTIVE MESSAGES
Define your goals.	Define your primary target audiences	Their concerns	What do they need to know or be assured of?	Prepare a set of four 'lead' messages

Tier Two Steps

THEME	REACTIVE MESSAGES	REFINE AND SIMPLIFY	TEST
Develop a theme which pulls together your messages	Brought out if specifically asked	Cut jargon - "retail" the message to your audience's everyday realities	Test your messages before delivering them (focus groups)

Tier Three Steps

POSITIONING STATEMENT	EXAMPLES, ILLUSTRATIONS and QUOTABLE QUOTES
Five or six sentences (30 seconds) to get started - could be background or summary of position on issue	

Communicate With Power™ Tier One Planning Tool

Goals:
1. _____
2. _____
3. _____

Audiences	Issues/ Concerns	Need to know/ Be assured of	Pro-active Messages
1			
2			
3			
4			

Communicate With Power™ Tier Two Planning Tool

Theme: _____

_____

Questions	Reactive Messages
1. _____	1. _____
2. _____	2. _____
3. _____	3. _____
4. _____	4. _____
5. _____	5. _____
6. _____	6. _____

Communicate With Power™ Tier Three Planning Tool

Positioning Statement	
Relate to Audience/Concern	
Major Challenge	
Goal	
Priority	
Proposal	
Major Benefit/Feature	

Examples
1. _____
2. _____

Anecdotes
1. _____
2. _____

Quotable Quotes
1. _____
2. _____

Presentation Planning Checklist

Date of Presentation: _____
Title: _____
Length of Presentation: _____
Location: _____
Room: _____
Time: _____
Organization: _____
Audience Size: _____
Contact Name: _____
Telephone: _____ Fax: _____ E-mail: _____
❏ Written Text   ❏ Point Form   ❏ Spontaneous

AV Requirements:
❏ Overhead Projector	❏ Acetates	❏ Markers
❏ 35mm Slide Projector	❏ Carousel	❏ Stack
❏ Screen	❏ Front Proj.	❏ Rear Proj.
❏ Computer	❏ Notebook	❏ Laptop
❏ Elect. White Board	❏ Video Proj.	❏ LCD Panel
❏ TV Camera	Format _____	
❏ VCR	Format _____	
❏ TV Monitor	Size _____	No. _____
❏ Remote(s)	❏ Laser Pointer	
❏ Flip Chart	❏ White Board	
❏ Podium	❏ Riser	

Microphone Type
❏ Clip-on (lavaliere)	❏ Neck	❏ Hand-held
❏ Podium	❏ Audience	No. _____
❏ Panel Members	No. _____	

Presentation Planning Checklist - cont'd

Room Set-up:
❏ Theater   ❏ U-shape   ❏ Hollow Sq.
❏ Tiered/Angled Tables ❏ Boardroom
Other_____

Supplies
❏ Hand-out Materials
Number Req'd:_____ Due: _____
❏ Note Pads
❏ Pencils
❏ Name Tags
❏ Registration List
Other
    ❏ _____
    ❏ _____
    ❏ _____
    ❏ _____
    ❏ _____
    ❏ _____

2 Prepare • *outline your presentation*

Outline Your Speech or Presentation

Now that you have analyzed your audience, identified your goals and defined your messages, you can begin to outline your presentation or speech. In doing so, it is important to realize that there are three parts to a successful presentation.

The Three Segments of a Speech or Presentation

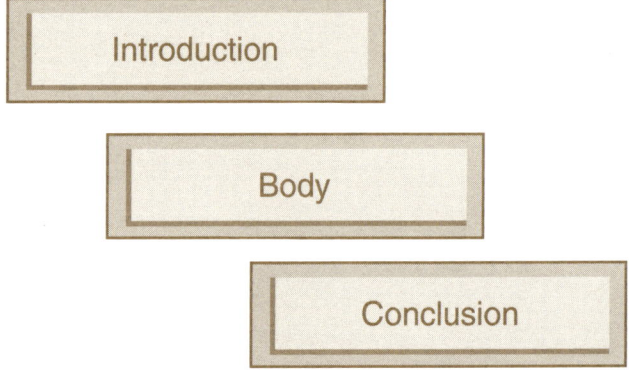

Introduction

Body

Conclusion

Introduction *(10% of presentation)*

- be sure to include:
  - Connection: to audience or issue - how does this speech fit in? Position the speech - is it a follow-up? a preamble?
  - Goal: state the overall purpose of your presentation
  - Outline: explain how you intend to achieve your goal
  - Motivation: answer the audience's question "What's in it for me" or "Why should I care about this?"
- the opening should:
  - set the tone
  - catch attention
  - put things in context
  - find a quick way to gain rapport
  - make a personal link or subject link to the audience
  - introduce the overall message
  - build a solid bridge between the audience and the topic

Ten Opening Tips

1. Visuals - visuals carry many times more power than words alone (consider photos, charts, models, slides, video).
2. Questions - most commonly these might include rhetorical questions posed only for thought or for you to answer. e.g. "How does the customer define service?" In an interactive, training-oriented presentation, pose the question directly to the audience and capture their replies on a screen or chart.
3. Tell the audience what you are not going to cover in your speech and why.
4. Quotation - works best if it is witty, relevant, opinionated, memorable, and said by a famous person.
5. Fact or Statistic - challenge or intrigue your audience.
6. Personal Touch - personal anecdote or incident which illustrates your focus point.
7. Self-Interest - appeal directly to your audience's own positive self-interest.
8. Begin with the central conclusion or overall message of your presentation.
9. Tell the audience what you are going to tell them.
10. Create suspense with music, spotlight and a voice-over announcer - supplemented by visuals flashing on the screen.

Final Pointers on Openings

- Don't take too long getting to the "meat" of the presentation.
- Eliminate a lot of "what I intend to share with you today…" or other verbal flourishes.
- Your opening remarks should be punchy, brief and give a sense of direction, priorities and vision.
- If you are delivering a formal speech from a written text, familiarize yourself with the introduction so that you don't have to read it.

Good evening. I for one am really looking forward to what I have to say…

 *(80% of presentation)*

The body contains the essence of your presentation. Build the body around the messages you have prepared. Utilize any of the planning tools outlined in this tab to help you structure the body of the presentation..

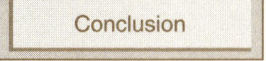

Conclusion *(10% of presentation)*

Always have a conclusion to pull your speech or presentation together.

Restate the overall message and repeat specific messages. If appropriate, make the conclusion motivational, uplifting. Use a relevant quote or joke to leave the audience thinking or laughing (preferably both). Answer the question, "So what?" In other words, what are the implications of your messages, for your audience, for a wider audience. Give a snapshot of the future, perhaps, or describe the "ultimate vision".

Don't say "thank you" at the end. The end of your speech should be evident in your delivery. Also, try to avoid "...so in summary..." or "in conclusion..." -it's redundant.

3 Design Visuals

- *presentation environments*
- *multimedia presentation*
- *how to add pizzazz*
- *choose the source; the display; the software*
- *creative hints*

Why Use Visuals?

43% more effective...

The Future...

...than without visuals.

Presentations That Use Visuals

The use of visuals increases the ability of the audience to understand and retain what you are saying. What you see, you remember.

The more senses you ask your audience to use - eyes, ears, touch, taste, smell - the more they will learn, retain and become motivated (of course, taste and smell may be pushing it...).

Presentation Environments

The objective, the audience and the room where the presentation takes place should dictate the appropriate technology for visual display.

Type 1: One-on-One Sales/Client Meeting

A table-top easel binder with a series of color visuals (laminated or contained in plastic sleeves) can be perfect for one-on-one informal, low-key client meetings. A color lap-top computer is ideal for a more polished, high-tech approach.

Type 2: Presenting Information or Animating Discussions - up to 30 participants
Computerized multimedia - using LCD projector panel or video projector; 35mm slides, overhead acetates (considered more 'audience-friendly' than slides), prepared flip-charts on easel boards.

Type 3: Presenting Information or Animating Discussion - from 30 to 150
Computerized multimedia - with LCD projector panel or video projector, 35 mm slides, overhead acetates. When animating a discussion with this size of group, capture audience suggestions on notebook computer or on overhead acetates.

Type 4: Large Formal Speech - 150 and up luncheon / dinner speech or presenting a symposium paper:
35 mm slide projectors, computerized multimedia with LCD projector panel or video projector.

Create a Multimedia Presentation

A multimedia presentation is a computer-based presentation which can combine a number of audio and video technologies, including:
- multimedia computer and/or LCD projection panel; LCD projector or video projector
- video cameras
- video disk player or VCR

The effects include:
- building a "stack" of slides displaying graphics, text, etc.
- animation
- video segments
- music, sound effects, audio voice-over

The benefits of multimedia include:
- access to thousands of still and moving images
- the capability of mixing graphic and video files in one screen while allowing the presenter to preview upcoming information
- the ability to move instantly to any prepared slide or video segment without being locked into a linear path.
- the ability to have a truly interactive presentation.

How to Add Pizzazz to Your Visuals

Computer-generated visuals have the capacity to add dynamic new elements to your presentation. These include:

- moving graphs which can show trends and charts unfolding before the audience
- animation of characters, objects etc.
- video of people, places and events (full-motion video requires enormous memory; however, even half-motion video can be very effective - your computer will require MPEG capability to digitally compress the visual information)

- sound effects can be used to punctuate graphics and visuals

What You Require

- A computer - preferably a notebook format - with significant hard drive memory; PC-MCIA diskette or a set of 1.4 MB floppy disks in an external cartridge; or CD-ROM. The CD-ROM has the memory capacity to offer full-motion video.
- A graphics software program which offers a range of visual options.
- Presentation hardware - such as an LCD projector panel and high-powered overhead projector; or video projector.
- A remote control to manage the presentation.

Choose the Source

1. Multimedia laptop or notebook computer - connected to LCD projector panel or video projector.
2. PowerMac® and Pentium® PC systems can run most presentation software, including multimedia packages - make sure you have sufficient internal memory (RAM) and hard disk storage to accommodate the operating system, your presentation program and the presentation files you will be producing.
3. Video - VCRs, video disk players and CD-ROM players (with up to 1.2GB memory on the CD-ROM disks to allow for video, graphics, animation and text combined).

Choose the Display

High Tech Solutions...

1. **Multimedia Video Projector**
   - stand-alone units which combine the LCD display, light source and projection optics
   - allows you to integrate multiple sources into a single easy-to-control projector
   - crisper images and more effective than LCD panels
   - can be used in lots of ambient light

2. **LCD Projector Panel**
   - flat devices, square or rectangular in shape, 1-2 inches thick, weighing about 7 lbs.; with about 8-10 inch screens (diagonally)
   - can project colorful output from both computer and video sources, at the same time if desired
   - requires high-intensity overhead projector (at least 4,000 lumens)
   - can project images up to 10 feet in size (diagonally)
   - some include built-in speaker

3. **Electronic White Board (for Windows® or Macintosh®)**
   - whatever you create on the board, appears instantly on your computer screen
   - once in the computer, you can save, print, cut, paste, e-mail, or fax it
   - ideal for collaborative discussions and brain-storming
   - great support tool for video conferences

Low Tech Solutions...

1. 35mm Slide Projector
- can present crisp, clear graphs, photographs, word charts
- ideal for a large audience (30-500), formal presentation
- requires a longer focal length between projector and screen than overhead projector

2. Overhead Projector
- high-intensity version can project true-color multi-media in normal light
- ideal for presentations to small-to-medium-sized audiences (10-30)
- readily available and highly interactive

3. Flip Chart/White Board
- old technology, but still valuable for small-group discussions, brainstorming sessions
- prepare flip chart pages (either manually or electronically) in advance for a more professional look

4. TV Monitor
- up to 40 inches (diagonally)
- can provide crisp visual output - ideal for boardroom presentations
- if two or more are connected together, they can be used for medium-sized audiences (up to 150)

Choose the Software

For slides and overheads: there are a range of software programs* that let you integrate text and graphics in individual slides, as well as sort and rearrange their sequence through built-in outliners. Also many contain transition effects along with the ability to add sound tracks and digital movies.

*   Software examples include: Adobe Persuasion® by Adobe Systems Inc.; Microsoft PowerPoint™ by Microsoft®; Software Publishing's Harvard Graphics® and ASAP®; Alpha Software's Bravo®; Corel Presentations™, CorelDRAW!™ and CorelFLOW™ by Corel®; Claris Impact® by Claris™; Lotus' Freelance Graphics™, and DeltaPrint's DeltaGraph® Pro to name a few.

Creative Hints for Visual Aids

Getting Started

Decide which ideas can be conveyed visually. Then sketch out your visuals roughly. Be creative and think visually. Plan an average of 1 to 2 visuals per minute of presentation time (this means that a 15 minute presentation would require between 15 and 30 visuals).

Tips for Slides

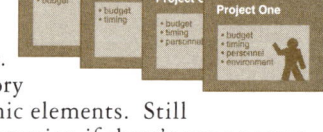

Some people prefer to read text.
Others stimulate their memory
with music. Some like graphic elements. Still
others can't connect the information if there's not a person
included. The solution? Try to reach everybody by varying
the visual elements without becoming too busy or having
the visuals dominate the message.

1. Limit the visuals to three or four colors throughout the
   presentation as too many colors will confuse the
   audience.
2. Use a common design element - avoid a smorgasbord
   of designs.
3. Each visual should have a message.
4. Never print words in red -very difficult to read.
5. Use photos, drawings, charts, pictorials.
6. Avoid too many word charts.
7. Use a minimum of 18 point font for text.
8. On average don't let a visual stay on for longer than 1
   minute. If you need longer, separate out the elements
   and "stack" them by adding additional points one at a
   time to build the full picture.
9. Use a blank slide or darkened screen if you're not
   continuing directly from one slide to another.
10. As a rule of thumb, use 1-2 visuals per minute of talk;
    unless the presentation is slide-driven (such as deliver-
    ing a paper at a symposium) in which case more visuals
    would be required.

11. Keep slides consistent; titles and copy should be the same colors and sizes.

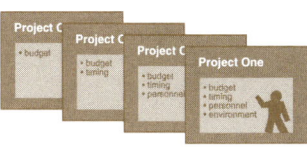

12. A background shaded in blue or green tends to work best.
13. Avoid using red and green together (color blindness is a common problem).
14. Try "stacking" a series of highlighted points to bring action to the presentation.
15. People love to look at pictures of other people, so try using people as a complement to text slides.

Linking the Messages

Now that you have your overall message, your specific messages, theme and you have sorted out the introduction, body and conclusion, you can begin to fill in the details.

Mini-Summaries: capsule messages that restate key points before a transition statement. e.g. "So in other words, significant savings can be achieved."

Transition: a phrase or sentence that shifts attention from previous subject or issue to the next:
- used at all major break points (introduction and body, between main points and between the body and conclusion)
- show logical connections
- recapture audience's attention
- clear up potential for confusion and make people feel comfortable

Example: "So, we are making progress on spending reductions. Now let's look at sharpening our market focus."

Crafting Your Opening - Making a Strong First Impression

- Prepare and practice your opening thoroughly, as this is the time you will be the most nervous.
- Make the first sentence brief and to the point. It could be the central message or main conclusion of your presentation.
- You could use a humorous opening remark or a brief anecdote - directly related to this speech.
- If you use humor, make sure it is appropriate, inoffensive, uncontrived and brief. It should suit the situation and be relevant either to the topic or to the person who introduced you.
- Try not to begin with an apology for anything (handouts, visuals, etc.) as this erodes the confidence of the audience, as well as your own.
- Goal statements are a good way to begin a presentation. e.g.: "I have one goal today. I want to persuade you to use the full range of services offered by our division."
- Indicate if questions should be asked during your presentation, at key points throughout it, or at the end.
- If not already known, let your audience know how long you anticipate the presentation will take.

Persuading an Audience

In order to persuade individuals or an audience to accept your idea, it is important to treat them as equal participants.

Persuasion is... finding mutually beneficial win/win outcomes, in which the audience starts to take ownership of the decisions made at each step.
Persuasion is not... manipulating or pressuring an audience.

One Persuasive Technique - Contrast Your Argument
Counterpoint: State the opposing positions on both sides.
Argument: Present your case, supporting your view, challenging the opposing views, or both. Or, position your argument as the one in the middle, or identify the other two positions as "the status quo" and "a variation of the status quo", while your position is targeted as one of change.

Persuasion: A Hierarchy of Communications

Grounding your arguments in values which have resonance with the audience serves to increase persuasiveness. Values have the capability of cancelling out the impact of prevailing attitudes. Attitudes, in turn, cancel out opinions.

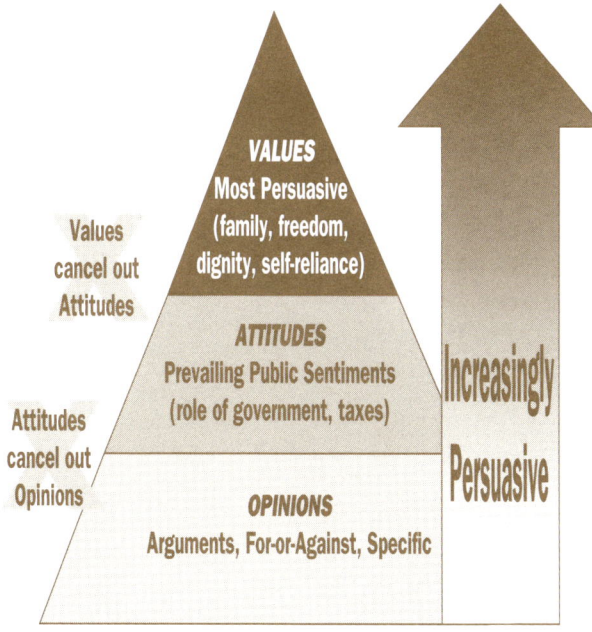

Values cancel out Attitudes

VALUES
Most Persuasive
(family, freedom, dignity, self-reliance)

ATTITUDES
Prevailing Public Sentiments
(role of government, taxes)

Attitudes cancel out Opinions

OPINIONS
Arguments, For-or-Against, Specific

Increasingly Persuasive

Another Technique... Rapport Builders

- find common ground immediately
- spotlight your "likeness" with the audience by stating mutual interests and sharing common experiences
- be fully responsive to audience problems/needs
- stay courteous towards everyone, no matter what the provocation
- emphasize the positives
- don't whitewash the negatives
- identify shortcomings of your position (note that "nothing is perfect")
- listen and feed back reflectively
- avoid pointless arguments
- be a problem-solver, not a salesperson
- call people respectfully by name when possible
- use gentle humor, where appropriate
- work for a WIN-WIN outcome

Building Bridges

Communicating that you are an excellent listener is a very powerful persuader. Bring into your presentation input from others who have spoken or written before you, then bridge to your own ideas.

Pacing your Presentation

The purpose of active pacing is to sustain the interest of the audience. Never rush your presentation. Take your time, feel the meaning behind the words. Think of your pace as replicating a dramatic film, as follows:

Introduction:
- begin to pick up pace
- hook the audience's interest
- surprise or challenge the audience

Body
- vary the pace throughout
- give specific details
- reach a crescendo of energy and enthusiasm

Conclusion
- slow down as you enter the conclusion phase
- begin to pick up the pace as you near the end
- summarize with energy

Pacing Tips

- keep changing the types and styles of visuals to maintain the audience's interest
- visuals should change from text to graphics to charts to photos
- switch technologies from slides to video to animation
- don't bog down in a rut; keep changing
- avoid a dizzying pace which leaves the audience confused and exhausted

Preparing Speaking Notes

- consider 4"x5" or 5"x7" cards with your speech laser-printed in 14pt text
- if using regular paper, end your notes ²/₃ of the way down the page - this will help you 'scoop' read the text
- number all pages or cards
- consider putting your speaking notes either under or above a miniature picture of your visuals (many presentation software packages offer this feature) - this way you'll always know where you are in the presentation
- carry your speaking notes in a speech box or have them at the podium before you speak.
- mark up the text by highlighting key words or phrases throughout your notes for emphasis
- indicate pauses - before key words, etc. (you could use double backslash // to signify a pause)
- at strategic points print reminders to yourself for eye contact, asking the audience if they have questions, etc.

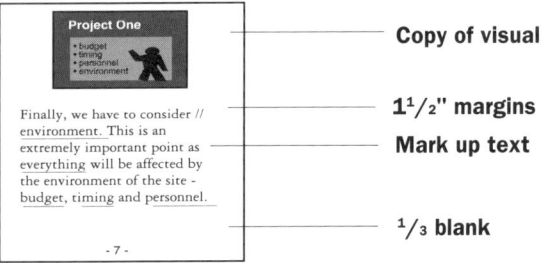

Scripting Your Speech

It has been said that the secret of writing is re-writing. Gertrude Stein once said, "I hate to write. I love having written." Another great writer said… "Writing is easy; all you do is sit down at the typewriter, open a vein and bleed." In other words, writing a speech is often agony - at minimum, difficult. Each word you write has the power to lift human hearts, create a sense of community and share vision, soothe or excite. Your words can send the audience into gales of laughter or bring them to tears (of course, those should be the intended outcomes!). Nothing replaces work, practice and… rewriting.

How to Get Started

Start your own collection of phrases, quotes and sentences that appeal to you and over the years you will fill a book with examples that move you. Practice taking one idea and re-working it until you feel you have expressed it with an economy of words and clear meaning and a dynamic rhythm. Then, keep practicing.

Punch Up Your Speech

- Use the active voice of verbs, not the passive
  "We are tackling this problem" not "The problem is being tackled."
- Use short sentences; don't bury your message in lengthy sentences. If you can edit out phrases and not lose the meaning of your message, do so.
- Use the inverted structure, in which the negative is stated first; followed by the positive. e.g. "Not pandering to the loudest voices but listening to those who have not been heard."
- Use visual metaphors or hooks which make your message more memorable.
  "One tiny ant can't do anything. But armies of ants can really get squashed. That's why I'm a fan of small teams."
- Use a 'triad' approach - ideas and words in groups of threes... e.g. "Hope over despair; action over inaction and, ultimately, success over failure."

How to Connect With the Audience

In order to sustain the mode of a "dialogue" try the following techniques:

- **Build in questions throughout your speech or presentation** - whether actual or merely rhetorical. The questions will engage the minds of the audience and prepare the ground well for your answers.
- **Keep your approach conversational** - mix in some humor, anecdotes, informal asides that are the hallmarks of conversation. The audience will feel they are being engaged genuinely, not merely treated as the recipients of a one-way transmission.
- **Tailor your speech**. Match your talk to the nuances and intricacies of the host organization. This will demonstrate to the audience that you a) care enough to become familiar with their concerns b) are approaching the subject from their perspective, c) are relating to them as individuals with unique experiences. As in any conversation, trying to understand the person you're speaking with makes it a much more meaningful experience.
- **Don't aim for perfection; just try to be authentic.** If you succeed in adopting a "dialogue" approach, the audience will forgive minor imperfections or flaws in your presentation delivery. If, however, you try to adopt a "perfection" approach, it will tend to come across as manufactured or phony.

Preparing Handouts

Consider providing a handout to support your speech or presentation. The handout could include: background reading, a copy of your visuals, biographies, reference material, etc.

Tips...

- consider distributing your handout after the presentation so that the audience will concentrate on your speech, rather than on the printed word
- make sure your name, department or organization are on the handout
- include a title page, with the name of the conference or audience, the date, etc.
- number the pages
- always have a copy of the handout close at hand when you are delivering your speech or presentation in case someone has a question or you wish to refer to a specific page

Deciding on Your Hand-Out Distribution Strategy

In Advance
- if necessary to read before the presentation or meeting
- if an important decision will be made and the audience needs to be well informed

At the Beginning of the Presentation
- if the audience will need to follow along in order to take notes
- if slides or visuals are used

During the Presentation
- only if it is important for the group to focus on a particular agenda item at a certain point
- if there is a surprise element

After the Presentation
- providing a hand-out on the way out adds further value to your speech without competing with the presentation for audience attention

5 Rehearse

- *run through*
- *vocal exercises*
- *breathing exercises*

Run-Throughs

Purposes

- familiarize yourself with the material
- pick out weak or missing links
- clarify meaning/ nuances
- improve delivery

Methods

- get feedback from objective observers
- if possible, video or audio tape your rehearsals
- playback with a critical eye and ear and watch for:
  - timing
  - tone
  - pace
  - vocal quality
  - continuity
- practice questions and answers to sharpen responses and instincts
- conduct three or four run-throughs to get comfortable with the material

Vocal Exercises

Speak From the Diaphragm

• Test if you are speaking from your diaphragm (located below your rib cage). Place your hand on your chest and say the alphabet aloud, elongating the sounds - aaaaa, beeeee, ceeeee, etc. You should feel your voice vibrating in your chest.

Pitch Exercise

• Apparently the average person speaks at a pitch level which is half an octave higher than his or her natural pitch. To find your natural pitch, do this exercise immediately before your speech:
  1. Count to 10 out loud in your normal pitch.
  2. Count to 10 using your highest pitch.
  3. Count to 10 in your lowest pitch while plugging your ears and shaking your head from side to side.
  4. Repeat this high and low counting for two minutes.
  5. Now count to ten in your natural pitch. You will find that your pitch will drop about half an octave.

Vary Your Inflection

Read the following statements aloud three times, each time emphasizing different words:
1. The single, greatest threat to self-sufficiency is despair.
2. The total contribution from all employees in every department has been truly magnificent.
3. Although technology can liberate us from mundane tasks, we must ensure that it does not restrict our creative imagination.
- Try singing first thing in the morning to develop a more melodic tone and give yourself a more upbeat mood.

Enunciation Practice

Say each three times, quickly:
1) Peter Piper picked a peck of pickled peppers. If Peter Piper picked a peck of pickled peppers, how many peppers did Peter Piper pick?
2) She sells seashells by the sea shore.
3) Six sick sheiks.
4) Rubber baby buggy bumpers.
5) How much wood could a woodchuck chuck if a woodchuck could chuck wood?
6) Good blood, bad blood.
7) Round the rugged rocks the ragged rascals ran.
8) Peggy Babcock packs bags.
9) Is this the path that passes to the south of the house?

Eliminate Uhs and Ums

Sit with someone and describe the room you are in. Have him or her clap sharply whenever you say "uh" or 'um". Keep going until you can do one minute without hearing the "clap" sound. Do this exercise several times in a row and watch how these barriers become less dominant.

During Your Presentation

- Sip water during a pause to keep your mouth lubricated.
- Practice full-lung breathing. As you breathe in during a pause, expand your stomach slowly. As you speak, slowly move your stomach inward to power your voice through to the end of your sentence. This will help you avoid volume trail-off at the end of sentences.
- Look to the audience members farthest from you, and speak in a conversational tone to avoid sounding harsh or coming across as yelling.

Dealing with Nervousness or Anxiety

Attacks of nervousness before a presentation are quite normal. Your pulse quickens, your blood flows to your body's core - leaving your feet and hands cold and clammy. Saliva dries up - leaving your mouth parched; butterflies form in your stomach... you're a wreck! There are key steps to take to make your nerves work for, rather than against you.

Relaxation Exercises

- Breathing
  - take 2 or 3 deep breaths to access your full lung capacity
  - do 2 or 3 minutes of slow, deep 'stomach' breathing
  - emphasize full breathing out
  - push stomach out, while breathing in
  - pull stomach in, while breathing out
- Loosening Up
  - tighten and relax your muscles starting from your feet and working your way up your body to your neck and shoulders
  - stomp your feet to get that 'grounded' feeling
  - shake your hands and arms loosely by your side
  - lean against a wall and push away, while holding your stomach in, making a hissing sound as you breathe out
  - make funny faces, rub your facial muscles along the jawline
  - rub around your eyes and along your forehead
- Limit yourself to 1 coffee - drink lukewarm water instead.
- Practice yawning which will open your throat.
- Chew gum, which will relax your jaw and tongue and keep the saliva flowing.

Psyche Yourself Up

- Clear your mind of all distractions and worries.
- Sit quietly and imagine yourself being successful, animated and confident before the group.
- Remind yourself of your expertise and strong points.
- Say to yourself: "I am confident, strong. I feel good about myself." Do not think negative thoughts about yourself or the audience.
- Give yourself this verbal cue: "I am going to have an interesting dialogue with a fascinating group of individuals." and "The audience is open-minded and interested in what I have to say."
- As you move toward the podium, your frame of mind will determine how dynamically and convincingly you deliver your presentation.
- If you think of the occasion as "delivering a speech" then you are not in the right frame of mind. That way of thinking implies one-way communications, with you the only one communicating. Guaranteed to make you uptight!
- Instead, deliberately imagine yourself engaging in an everyday activity in which all of us feel comfortable participating — a two-way dialogue.
- Think of your presentation as animating or being engaged in a stimulating conversation or dialogue... even though you might be the only one speaking!

- *special situations*
- *verbals*
- *para-verbals*
- *non-verbals*
- *making an entrance*
- *dress and appearance*

Your Delivery Goals

- Get your message across.
- Drive the energy in the room.
- Re-create the aura of a dynamic, two-way conversation.
- Generate enthusiasm; spark fresh thinking in the audience.
- Communicate confidence and poise.
- Get buy-in to your idea or proposal.

Special Situations

If Your Mind Goes Blank...

- Don't panic. Take a deep breath. Be seen to pause and think.
- Try to pick up a linking or bridging phrase, such as "Let me move on."
- Or, if it's only a minor point that you've forgotten, admit your mind has gone blank and move on! "I've got a great memory... it's just short!"
- Don't begin a sentence until you know what you want to say - otherwise it will be painfully obvious that you are 'stuck'.
- Don't keep thinking about the forgotten point. It will erode the effectiveness of the remainder of your presentation.
- Remind yourself that the audience doesn't really know if you've missed a point or two.
- Remember, your goal is not to be perfect, but to be authentic. It's not a major problem to go blank. The damage comes in how you handle it. Don't spend an embarrassing amount of time trying to recall your point. Show wit and humor and poise as you deal with an all too human reality.

If You Can't Begin Due to Audience Inattention...

- Stay quiet and look at those who are creating most of the noise. This will encourage nearby audience members to ask them to quiet down.
- Look like you want to start. Adjust the microphone. Stack your cards or notes together.
- Smile at the offending audience members and raise your eyebrows.
- If all else fails, begin speaking. "Ladies and gentlemen"... (pause) "Ladies and gentlemen."... "If we could just have my attention please"... (smile) Look at your watch and say... "we're running a little late..." then slowly move into your speech.
- Never show anger with your audience. It will destroy the atmosphere for the rest of your speech.
- If you are still being ignored...

Verbal Elements

Pitch
In most cases, use your normal pitch which is a half-octave lower than the everyday range of your voice. Your voice should sound resonant, not reedy or tight. (See Vocal Exercises.)

Pace
Too fast or too slow will frustrate the audience. Vary the pace to keep it interesting.

Inflection
Vary the tone of your voice by raising and lowering the inflection throughout your speech. e.g. "To those who say we should do nothing (rising), I say that is a policy of despair (falling)". Avoid ending a sentence on a rising up-tone. It sounds uncertain? Questioning?

Emphasis
Underscore key words and phrases to build in pauses and provide some interest. Varying the emphasis you place on words helps to draw attention to key concepts and avoid tedious, monotone delivery.

Volume
Your voice should fill the room without yelling. Speak from the diaphragm (space below your rib cage) rather than from your larynx (voice box). Speak to the person in the back row.

Pauses
Pausing before or after key words emphasizes importance and communicates thoughtfulness.

Vocabulary
Clear, everyday language is essential to understanding. Avoid jargon, "bureaucratese" or a highly technical vocabulary.

Sentence Length
Don't bore the audience with run-on sentences. Shorter, punchier sentences are easier to understand and will make your message stand out.

Energy
Ultimately it is the energy you project about the subject which audiences remember. Don't let the volume peter out at the end of sentences.

Articulate
Open your mouth up and pronounce each word clearly. Don't slur words.

Remember...

Use your natural voice which should sound comfortable and pleasant. Your goal is to sound animated and energized.

Vocabulary
Avoid pedantic or overused phrases
- "It is indeed a pleasure to be here today."
- "On the one hand…"
- "If the truth be known…"
- "The bottom line is…"
- "We're stuck between a rock and a hard place."
- "If I can just be serious for a moment…"
- "Let me be perfectly clear…"
- "Having said that…"
- "That reminds me of a funny story…"
- "Don't tell the boss, but…"
- "To be completely honest…"
- "Economics-wise…"

Choosing Your Vocabulary

1. Don't talk over the heads of your audience. Jargon is a killer of effective communications. If you feel you have to use jargon, signal it humorously - "Jargon alert" - then use the word - and define it.
2. Not all words have equal value. Some words have far more emotion or resonance attached to them than others. This can work for or against you, so be aware of the nuances. For example, "enemies" is a powerfully negative word, whereas "adversaries" communicates a less paranoid tone.
3. Visual language is more memorable than technical or imprecise language. e.g.. "A driving force in history..." rather than "One of the common elements of history..."
4. Don't repeat needless words or phrases which clutter up the speech such as "for one thing...", "that is to say", "in fact", "indeed".
5. Use color words with visual connotations and impact. e.g. "devastating", "shattered", "crucial", "exploding".

Use of Humor

A delicate art. If it works, it can be the perfect ice-breaker. Start a collection of your own humorous lines which you can call upon for spontaneous speeches, toasts, and so on.

Tips...

- Be sure that you are reinforcing your main focus.
- The humor must be appropriate and in good taste.
- The butt of the joke (if there is one) is you, not anyone else.
- Keep it low key.
- Don't laugh at your own jokes.
- Don't telegraph the punchline - keep a straight face.
- Don't force the humor - it should flow naturally from the situation or the subject.
- Keep it brief - the longer your attempt to be funnier, the more hilarious it better be.
- If it doesn't get a laugh - don't blame the audience.

Para-Verbal Elements

Tone and Attitude:
Keep the tone warm and engaging.

Stay away from sounding:
- smug
- arrogant
- hostile
- defensive
- uptight
- negative
- trying too hard to please

Focus on projecting that you are:
- modest
- reasonable
- open
- relaxed
- friendly
- positive
- confident

Non-Verbal Elements

When John F. Kennedy debated Richard Nixon on television in 1960, the majority of viewers were most swayed by the calm, cool, collected appearance of Kennedy. The majority of those who listened on the radio, however, were more impressed with Nixon's performance. The lesson is, though, that non-verbals tend to dominate the verbal message.

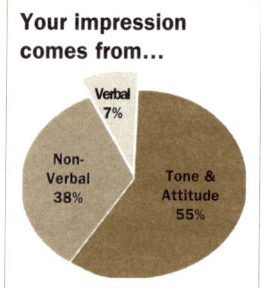

Your impression comes from...

Verbal 7%

Non-Verbal 38%

Tone & Attitude 55%

Closed...
You do not want to communicate closed body language which sends the message "closed-off and uptight":

- arms folded across the chest
- face tight
- eyes narrowing
- muscles tense
- shoulders hunched
- tightly gripping and 'straight-arming' the podium

Open...
Instead, communicate open body language which signals that you are comfortable with yourself and your message and that you are open to feedback:

- shoulders back and down
- arms and hands open
- face animated and friendly
- strong eye contact
- fluid gestures

While You are Introduced

If you are on stage or within eye contact of the audience while you are being introduced, all eyes will be on you and not the person introducing you. Therefore...

Dos...

- Look at the person who is introducing you in an open, affirmative way.
- Smile appropriately, even if the joke is not that funny.
- Sit (or stand) confidently, with open body language.
- Animate your face.

Don'ts...

- If the humor is racist, sexist, etc. do not smile, as the audience may think you condone such beliefs.
- Don't look bored, indifferent, tense or uncertain.
- Don't stare at the audience or off into space.

Making an Entrance

An audience forms an initial impression of you from the first time they see you. Try to communicate warmth and confidence through your body language.

- If you are going to wear a clip-on or neck microphone, make sure it's already attached before you are introduced. There is nothing worse than to be fumbling with a microphone while an audience watches. Don't activate the transmitter until you are "on".

- Smile when you are introduced and walk purposefully, yet with a relaxed walk, to the podium (or to the front of the room). If you have notes, either have them placed neatly into a speech box or have them at the podium in advance. If you have cards, place them deliberately on the podium just before starting.

- When you look out at the audience, do so deliberately, not furtively and hold for a few seconds before beginning.

How to Adjust the Podium Microphone

(preferably before your audience arrives)

- Place one hand firmly on the lower part of the microphone stand (assuming it's the flexible kind) and place the other firmly on the upper end of the stand. Moving both hands, angle the microphone so that it is about 6 - 8 inches (13 to 18 cm.) from your mouth at approximately a 45° angle.
- Take your time and don't talk while adjusting it. If it does go on for an embarrassing length of time, you could break the tension with a line, such as, "They promised me there would be no physical labor..." or "I draw the line at windows..."
- Never tap the microphone and ask "Is this on?"

Using a Microphone

- Don't lean into the microphone... if the microphone is set up properly, it won't be necessary.
- Speak from the diaphragm; not from the throat. In that way you get a fuller, more resonant sound. Never yell to be heard.
- Project your voice so that you can be heard in the back row. If you or the organizers are unable to personally check the sound system, ask those in the back or "the price-challenged seats" if they can hear you. They'll soon tell you.
- As you raise the volume of your voice, do not sacrifice the inflection and pacing that creates the aura of an "energized conversation".
- Listen to yourself as you speak. Keep asking yourself, does my tone of voice sound spontaneous or conversational? If not, adjust appropriately.
- If you are getting audio feedback and there is no audio engineer, start by moving the microphone back slightly from your mouth. If that doesn't work, move away from the place where the feedback was most noticeable. Often feedback is caused by two audio sources which are too near each other.
- If using a hand-held microphone, maintain the same distance and angle all the way through your talk. Again about six inches (13 cm) should be sufficient.

How to Stand

- Straight, but not stiff. Shoulders back and down.
- Place your feet about 12 inches (30 cm) apart.
- Put your weight on the balls of your feet; don't lean back on your heels.
- Don't sway from side to side. If you have a side-to-side swaying tendency, put one foot slightly in front of the other.
- If you sway back and forth, ensure that your feet are placed evenly beside each other - not one in front of the other.
- If the presentation is informal, don't wander around while talking. Move, stop, then talk.
- If there is a podium, don't lean on it. Place your hands lightly on the top.
- Never rest on the podium.

Optional Stances - without a podium

- Finger tips touching, waist-high, pointing down.
- Palm of one hand on top of the other.
- One hand in your pocket occasionally. Do not ever jingle the change in your pocket.

Where to Stand When Using Visual Support

An Informal Presentation

While screen is in use, move to one side and back towards the edge of the screen.

Formal Presentation or Speech

Place the screen off to one side, or stand between two screens.

Tips...

- never turn your back on the audience
- don't block the screen
- if making an informal presentation, stand beside the screen and look out towards the audience - only glancing at the screen occasionally

Using Your Hands

- Do what you feel comfortable with, but don't be distracting.
- Use your hands to emphasize a point or to provide visual logic to accompany your speech.
- Don't overuse your hands. Use them occasionally, and only for a reason - not just for the sake of it.
- Make specific gestures, not half-hearted, repetitive or distracting ones.
- Make your gestures compact, dynamic and complete.
- Let the gesture precede the word by a fraction.
- Never point your finger at an audience.

Facial Expression

- Smile! Not just when something is funny, but when talking about opportunities, challenges, etc. (don't over do it though).
- Raise your eyebrows and change expressions to animate your face.
- Look thoughtful and serious when you are talking about serious concerns.
- Concentrate on looking open and receptive, not closed-off and expressionless.

Ten Practical Tips on Eye Contact

1. **Make it real.** Dynamic eye contact is direct, one-to-one, and genuine.

2. **Stay focused.** Don't let your eyes flit around too quickly. Stop to really look at people in your audience long enough to register understanding with each one.

3. **Keep moving.** Look, but don't stare down your audience. If you look at any one person for too long, you'll both start to feel uncomfortable and, at some point, your target may get irritated or hostile.

4. **Use variety.** Don't look your audience over in a mechanical "radar sweep" motion. Keep your eye contact random and natural.

5. **Stay involved.** Ignore the disastrous advice to "look at a spot in the back of the room". Look at the people in the audience.

6. **Build rapport.** If you're shy or nervous, beware of a natural tendency to avoid eye contact. To others, a total lack of eye contact by you is a signal to distrust your words.

7. **Include everyone in the audience.** You may tend to talk only to friendlier faces. Force yourself to include everyone.

8. **Keep eye contact** with the audience even if delivering from a written text. (Try the 'scoop reading' technique described in this booklet).

9. When using visual aids, remember to **keep eye contact with the audience**, not the screen, flip chart, etc.

10. **Open and close well**. Give your audience especially full eye contact at the two most critical parts of the presentation - the opening and closing. If it helps, write the words "EYE CONTACT" into your notes as a reminder.

Handling Visual Aids

1. Don't pick up your visual until you're ready to use it.
2. Place the visual so that everyone can see it.
3. Hold visuals so that they don't hide your face.
4. Talk to the audience, not to the visual.
5. Put the visual aside when you're through with it.
6. Don't cover part of a transparency, then "reveal" it… it can be a distraction or even annoying.
7. If your hands shake - don't use a pointer. If you're using an overhead projector, place your pen on the projector, pointing out what you need to. Pick it up when you're through.
8. Turn off the projector while answering questions, when finished, or to refocus attention on yourself.
9. Position yourself to one side of the screen, facing the audience when using slides or overheads.
10. For Formal Speeches
    • 35 mm slides provide the most effective visual support to a formal speech.
    • Slides may be either front or rear screen projected (rear-screen projection requires that slides be inserted into the tray in reverse of front-screen projected slides).
    • It is relatively simple, yet highly effective, to use 2 or more projectors operating in tandem. For example, one projector could project a visual while the other projects text.

Dress and Appearance

For Men:

- Avoid three-piece suits. They tend to look stuffy and overly formal.
- Don't wear black suits; they project a lack of trust.
- Avoid extremes of color, pattern or style. Conservative styles in the median range of colors — greys and blues in particular — enhance your image. Navy blue is the most flattering color for almost everyone except men who are very fair or light-skinned (in which case, try charcoal grey).
- Stay away from busy patterns in clothing or short-sleeved shirts.
- Wear a white or pale blue shirt, or one with stripes.
- Wear a tie that has a strong color, such as burgundy, to reflect color into your face. Make sure the tie touches your belt buckle and is straight.
- A beard or mustache lowers the trust level and can communicate a stern image. If you can't part with your beard or mustache, make sure it is well-groomed and doesn't cover your upper lip. A beard or mustache restricts the range of facial expression, so compensate with even more facial animation.

Choosing the Appropriate Clothing - Men

- A well-tailored blue or charcoal-gray suit is ideal for formal speeches and presentations.
- If you are somewhere "in the middle" about your desired image, a navy blue blazer and coordinated pants work well (grey in the fall/ winter/spring and tan in the summer).
- A bow tie can communicate an academic, professorial look.
- A sport coat and tie conveys a more casual look than a suit and should only be worn in an informal setting.
- A blue denim or plaid shirt communicates a relaxed, comfortable and warm image - only for informal, casual gatherings.
- Dress one step up from the audience, never one step below.
- Always be well-groomed.
- Don't wear a button-down shirt with a double-breasted blazer or coat.
- Never wear socks which are a lighter color than your suit.
- Wear pure fabrics... 100% cotton shirts, silk ties and 100% wool suits.
- Look in the mirror for a last-minute grooming check-up.

Dress and Appearance

For Women:

- Avoid extremely short skirts.
- Strong jewel colors project confidence: e.g. royal blue, ruby red, emerald green and purple.
- Wear bright colors on top with a darker color on bottom such as a red jacket with a black or navy skirt.
- A jacket and skirt combination or a well-tailored dress are most flattering.
- Keep jewelry to a minimum.
- Avoid pure white blouses (unless worn with a jacket).
- Keep hair off your face; hair spray can be very helpful.

Overall Dress and Appearance Tips - Men and Women

- Remember, clothing can reinforce your message and tone and project self-confidence or, conversely, can cancel out your message and undermine your credibility.
- Don't let your clothes distract from your message.
- If you must wear glasses, choose non-reflective lenses. If you really don't need them for the speech, and if you feel comfortable without, then don't keep putting them on and taking them off.
- If you need to wear glasses, avoid the half-frame style, or ones that block the view of your eyes.

10 Presentation Skills Reminders

1. Do 3 minutes of deep-breathing exercises and 5 minutes of vocal exercises.
2. Speak from the diaphragm, not the throat.
3. If using a microphone don't "shout it out". Instead, concentrate on communicating a warm, spontaneous tone.
4. Smile, animate your face a lot.
5. Use your hands for emphasis - get into the speech physically.
6. Don't memorize - "scoop read" your text.
7. Eliminate the phrase: "I think" as well as "uh" and "um" sounds.
8. Change tone throughout the speech.
9. Try to begin with a spontaneous opening.
10. Have fun with it.

- *Spontaneous Presentations*
- *Preparing a Presentation Quickly*
- *Formal Speeches*
- *Panel Discussions*
- *Making Introductions*
- *Making and Responding to Toasts*
- *Corporate Videos*
- *Teleprompter® Use*
- *Client Presentations*
- *Product Demonstrations*

Delivering a Spontaneous Presentation

When you are asked, without prior notice, to deliver an impromptu or off-the-cuff presentation, does it mean… "Spontaneous Combustion" or "Spontaneous Excellence"?

Key Tips…

- **Pause first** to collect your thoughts. It also builds a little suspense. Pausing demonstrates that you are giving considered thought to the subject.
- **Pause several times** during your presentation in order to give yourself time to think.
- Demonstrate that you are an organized thinker. Approach the subject in an organized, clear manner. **Provide structure** to your comments, possibly as follows:
  - bridge over from a previous speaker's comments, e.g. "Bill brought up a point earlier which I would like to address…"
  - state succinctly the issue being explored or addressed

- identify the principle(s) which are important to consider
- break out each principle or issue separately and bring to bear some ideas, thoughts, or suggestions on each one
- draw conclusion(s)

- **Move the discussion forward**. Never be seen to bog down in detail or endless minutiae.
- **Be a good listener**. Refer to previous remarks by other participants in prior meetings.
- **Speak slowly and clearly.**
- **Build bridges** throughout your presentation to other positions and advocates - even if they are in opposition to yours.
- **Pose rhetorical questions** which frame your remarks - especially effective when you don't have a lot of answers.
- **Add self-deprecating humor** to your presentation, if appropriate.
- **Keep it brief** - never more than 2-3 minutes in a meeting format and never more than 7-8 minutes in a stand-up spontaneous speech or presentation.
- **Maintain strong eye contact** with each individual (if in a meeting) or each section of the audience (if a group presentation).
- **Animate your face.** Smile! Vary your facial expression as appropriate. Raise your eyebrows to maintain an open, friendly face.

Preparing a Presentation Quickly

List half a dozen key questions about the subject that the audience would have on their minds. Present each question, then answer it. Allocate time for each question and answer so you will be able to time your presentation - remember to leave time for audience questions.

Sample questions...

1. What do we mean by "this subject"?
2. What is it not? (common misconceptions)
3. What will it mean to the audience (opportunities, dangers, challenges)?
4. What are the consequences of not proceeding?
5. What are the options?
6. What do I recommend?
7. Why? (key benefits)
8. What are the implications for the audience?

Presentations Without a Prepared Text

With informal presentations, don't read from a prepared text. Instead, you could use the visuals on the screen to prompt you. Remember to "add value" to a visual through embellishing the points. Never just read a visual - it's patronizing and annoying to an audience.

More tips...

- If you don't have sufficient visuals to prompt you, use 5 x 7 cards with key words.
- Prepare quotes and statistics that are easy to grasp (i.e. nothing complicated).
- Watch for "uh" sounds (and other verbal barriers such as "like", "ok", "um", "basically", etc.). Build in pauses instead.
- Make the speech sound like an energized, informal dialogue with the audience.
- Practice so that it flows more fluidly each time.

Delivering a Speech from a Written Text

Your goal is to take ownership of the words on the page. Therefore, avoid the "watch-me-read-this-speech" syndrome. To accomplish this, try "scoop reading" your speech.

Scoop Reading

- Glance down, pick up 5-6 words, look up and deliver to your audience.
- Only use up three quarters of each page to make "scoop reading" easier.
- Limit each line of text to a "scoopable" amount.
- Make sure your notes are scripted in simple, informal language with brief sentences.
- Mark the text to help you break up the phrases for scoop reading.
- Underline words to emphasize, and indicate pauses.
- Don't sound like you're reading. Try to sound spontaneous by making maximum eye contact with the audience and by varying your tone and inflection.
- Don't deliver the words while looking down.
- After you finish one phrase, glance down and grab another.
- Balance your eye contact to 80% to the audience, 20% at the text.

Panel Discussions

Steps for a Moderator

1. Introduce yourself.
2. Set the climate, tone.
3. State the objectives.
4. Introduce the panel members.
5. Establish the ground rules and agenda.
6. Give panel members a time limit for each presentation - 5 minutes suggested.
7. Call for questions from the floor.
8. Direct the flow of questions; clarify if necessary.
9. Wrap up/conclusion.
10. Thank the panel and the group.

If You Are a Panel Member

Plan... make sure you know the purpose, ground rules, who your fellow panel members are, background on them and their views; information on the sponsoring organization, audience members, interesting tidbits which the audience would know, etc.

Prepare... a five minute presentation with a maximum of 3 key messages and relate them to the target audience and theme. Save something for the discussion - don't put all your points into the presentation part.

Also prepare visual support appropriate to your presentation (or provide visuals and background in hand-out notes).

Rehearse... your presentation so that it is punchy and distilled.

During the Panel Discussion...

- Be gracious and polite, even if attacked by a fellow panel member or audience member.
- Relate to what your fellow panel members have said.
- Try to define the issue to be addressed - thus encouraging the others to respond to you.
- Directly engage your fellow panel members - if the rules allow.

Responding to Audience Questions...

- Ask for, or listen for, the name of the questioner and use it.
- Try for a win/win response, limiting yourself to 60 seconds:
    - empathize or relate at the outset of your answer (10 seconds)
    - give a clear message (10 seconds)
    - support it with one or two points/facts (30 seconds)
    - give a one-line summary or re-statement of message (10 seconds)

Responding to Contributions From Other Panel Members

- Have fun - be direct - poke fun at yourself.
- Be a good sport - don't twist their words or attack them.
- Try to find something to agree with as well as points where you differ.

Introducing a Speaker

If you are asked to introduce a guest speaker, take it seriously and put some work into doing it well.

Goals of an Introduction

1. Position the issue - why is this important?
2. Introduce the guest speaker - credentials relative to the subject or organization.
3. Create interest in the audience.

Ten Tips for Introducing a Speaker

1. Avoid clichés, such as "…someone who needs no introduction…"
2. Try to build in some common element between the speaker's background, experience, accomplishments, etc. and your audience.
3. Don't take more than two minutes.
4. Don't get carried away with embellishments or it will be embarrassing to the speaker (and to you).
5. Don't go all the way through his or her resumé. Pick out some aspect of it which you found interesting, curious or "odd". This gives the guest speaker a chance to begin spontaneously by picking up on that reference.
6. Quote a famous person and link that quote to the speaker. e.g. "I believe it was Albert Einstein who once said, "Imagination is more powerful than intelligence." Today, we have a guest who has demonstrated both imagination and intelligence…"
7. Build in a little humor, aimed at yourself or the subject matter, but not at the expense of your guest.
8. Leave the name of the guest until part-way into your introduction. This builds suspense.
9. Think of a three-step structure to your introduction:
   • Why the subject is important
   • Who the guest speaker is… credentials and then name.
   • How the speaker's topic fits with the theme and/or the audience's needs and interests.
10. A good introduction should sound sincere and generate enthusiasm without making you the center of attention.

Thanking a Speaker

A public thank-you to a guest speaker is a work of art. It requires you to pay attention to what he or she has said, and reflect back to the audience the meaning you are taking away from the presentation.

Tips

1. Take some notes during the presentation - themes and messages particularly.
2. Weave references to them into your thank-you.
3. Keep your thank-you speech to one minute.
4. Keep the tone light and upbeat.
5. Be sincere as you thank the speaker on behalf of everyone.
6. A token of appreciation (if appropriate for outside speakers) is often the best way to demonstrate that sincerity. (The present does not have to be opened in front of the audience.)

Making Toasts

- If possible, prepare your toast in advance and practice it before the event.
- Remember your audience when you make a toast and don't speak over their heads or make off-color remarks.
- Smile, engage the audience, animate your face.
- Always stand when you give a toast.
- Make sure you have the audience's attention - most people will strike a glass with a spoon and say "If I may have your attention…"
- Speak loudly and clearly.
- If you are unknown to some of the audience, state your name and your relationship to the person or organization being toasted.
- Limit a toast to a maximum of 60 seconds - you are not making a speech when you make a toast.
- Find a way to include the audience or your fellow guests in the spirit of the toast.
- Adding a relevant quote from a famous person or from a significant event can add a touch of class to the toast.
- If you wish to use humor, use a self-deprecating approach.
- You must have a glass with something in it (some people consider toasting with water to be bad luck) in order to make a toast.
- It must be clear that the toast is over and that the audience may now drink, you could try "so please join me…"
- You must drink the toast.

Responding to Toasts

- Thank the person who toasted you and make a reference to how the two of you have related in the past.
- Keep the response short.
- Always have a quote or two prepared which you can use to elevate the tone of your response.
- If appropriate for the occasion, make it clear that you are responding with a toast; don't just say a few complimentary things and drink - the word 'toast' should be used.
- The audience should not be left guessing as to what you are doing, when it's over, when to drink or when to continue with their meal, etc.
- The acceptable limit for a response is approximately 60 seconds.

Corporate Videos

With the power of closed circuit television, computer networks, desktop video technology or video-taped programs to reach vast numbers of people, the ability to master the video medium is more important than ever.

Purposes

There are a number of purposes to video programs:
- employee video newsletters - regular (often monthly or quarterly) in the form of video news magazines
- corporate videos highlighting or explaining initiatives or events
- live video-conferenced announcements

If you have limited time to prepare, a teleprompter® may be necessary.

Using a Teleprompter®

Teleprompters® are used in major presentations, televised events, in hosting corporate videos, advertising, etc. The teleprompter® consists of a computer, software and one or two monitors. The operator of the teleprompter® makes sure that the text flows at a rate which keeps pace with you as you deliver your speech. Used correctly, a teleprompter® will give the audience the impression that you are looking at them and delivering your speech without any written notes.

Tips

- Make sure the operator is familiar with your pace of delivery and can keep up to you.
- Check that you can clearly see the text as it scrolls on the teleprompter® screen. The screen can be angled up or down or side to side.
- Look into the center of the line of text - try not to have your eyes notably shifting from left to right. This is especially important when making a video presentation.
- Have your text formatted with only five to seven words per line to help you with scoop reading.
- Speak in an informal tone.
- Work hard on sounding spontaneous, rather than sounding like a mechanical reader; vary the inflection widely.

- Practice with the teleprompter® operator a few times so that the pace of delivery matches the scrolling text. Remember that you control the pacing of the teleprompter®, not the operator.
- Try to break up the static shot by shifting from one teleprompter® screen to another, using video clips, changing the setting, getting up and walking over to an object or to a "guest" or just turning to another camera for a new sequence. Building in edit points like these means if you make a mistake, you don't have to start over from the very beginning.
- Keep a hard copy of your speaking notes on the podium or desk in front of you and slide one page over the other as you complete it. This is very important in case a technical glitch with the tel-eprompter® leaves you stranded. In order to coordi-nate it, make sure that the page number is placed onto the bottom of each page displayed on the teleprompter®.
- If using a teleprompter® system to deliver a speech, you will be using two video screens. Practice a fluid transfer from one screen to the next. For example, begin delivering a sentence from one screen and halfway through shift to the other until the sentence is complete. Then glance down at your notes (with-out looking at them specifically) look up and deliver to the first screen. In this way the audience can't tell if you are reading from a teleprompter® or not. Vary this pattern regularly so it doesn't become obvious or mechanical.

Client Presentations

Meeting with a client is an important occasion which may not include a formal presentation, but nevertheless has an undercurrent set of messages. The same careful preparation for a formal presentation should go into a meeting.

Pre-Meeting

- Find out if you will be meeting the final decision-maker.
- Find out what your customer's needs really are.
- Prepare your presentation.
- Know your messages and your facts.
- Talk to others in your organization who may have special insight into this client.
- If you have special A/V requirements, double check in advance to make sure they are available, operational and that you are confident in using them (practice).
- Agree in advance on the objectives, time frame and agenda.
- If a decision is to be made, make sure the client has the appropriate documentation in advance.
- Confirm the time and location the day before.
- Don't think of 'selling'; think of getting "client buy-in".
- Practice several times.

Making a Client Presentation

- Shake hands firmly and warmly.
- Communicate a friendly, open and engaging manner.
- Limit small talk to 2 minutes, then fall silent and let the client take the lead.
- Practice active listening with your eyes, face and ears.
- Encourage the client to speak.
- Reaffirm objectives for the meeting at the outset — get client buy-in.
- Match the benefits of your product or service to your client's needs — get client buy-in at each stage.
- Ask for input, questions, etc.
- Seek clarity if the client is vague.
- If appropriate, close the deal — ask for sale, approval, etc.
- Summarize what was agreed upon and confirm the next steps.

Making Product Demonstrations (Trade Shows, etc.)

Keys to Successful Demonstrations...

- Catch the interest of the crowd: ask them about their interests first.
- Have a prepared list of questions which could be asked, and be familiar with the answers (make them available as hand-outs).
- Stress the key benefits of the product.
- Practice using the product until you are an expert.
- Convey the sense that you enjoy using the product.
- Smile! Have fun.
- Try to be sincere, not glib or slick.
- Take breaks every hour to rest your voice and stay fresh.
- Give the prospects in front of you 100% of your attention; make them feel they are respected, liked and valued.
- If the prospect is qualified (you determine they are genuinely interested in the product but aren't going to buy at the show), obtain information from them (name, address, phone, fax, e-mail, etc.) so that you can follow-up after the show.
- Ask everybody you talk with to leave their cards for your database.
- Follow-up after the show-with special attention to those whom you promised specific information, with a general mailing to everyone else.

Don'ts...

- Don't disengage if you don't have any prospects around you - stay alert, relaxed and confident.
- Don't eat at your booth. The smell and sight can be a real turn-off, and some prospects just do not like interrupting a meal.
- Don't sit down; you are there to work the show and that means being up on your feet and talking to prospects.
- Don't neglect your booth - keep it neat, clean, and well-stocked with brochures and products.
- Don't wait for prospects to pick up a brochure; hand them one and engage their interest.

- *appearing before a committee*
- *planning and conducting effective meetings*
- *creating a win-win atmosphere*
- *vocabulary & skills for effective meetings*
- *thinking clearly*
- *gaining consensus and negotiating*

Appearing Before a Committee

Key Types of Committees

1. **Legislative** - examining legislation, special or select committee to study an issue.
2. **Public Inquiry** - to examine an incident, event or issue - primarily for fact-finding and to make recommendations, usually to a legislative body.
3. **Regulatory Commission** - public hearings to award or deny license, address regulatory issue relevant to industry and/or consumers.
4. **Judicial Inquiry** - features sworn witnesses, convened to find evidence of wrong-doing.

Mr. Chairman, could the committee just watch me read my opening statement, agree with me immediately and get it over with?

Your Goals in Appearing Before a Committee...

1. Set Out the Facts - as objectively as possible.
2. Communicate Credibility - by being fair-minded, projecting a tone that is reasonable, sincere and warm.
3. Get Your Messages Across - your overall message plus up to three specific messages (see the Plan and Prepare Tab).
4. Respond to Committee Questions - by giving direct, straight-forward answers to members' questions you help your case enormously.
5. Stay Cool - no matter the provocation, never lose your temper when testifying. You come across as out-of-control and extreme.

Preparing Your Opening Statement...

1. **Know your purpose.** Ask "What am I trying to achieve?" and write the answer down on your notes. This will help you keep perspective during your appearance.

2. **Know your committee** - study issues or concerns that could be relevant to your appearance. Also, study each member's history, opinions, district which could impact on your subject.

3. **Find out in advance** from the clerk of the hearing:
    i)   the desired length or time of your oral statement;
    ii)   if a written statement is required in advance for circulation to Committee Members;
    iii) if you are able to provide a detailed written statement with a shorter oral version to high-light the key points, and
    iv)   if audio-visual support is allowable and, if so, the limitations.

4. **Draft a 3-sentence version of your statement.** This will form the essence of your entire presentation. Aim your entire opening statement towards that 3-sentence version. It should be focused on the overall message and the three specific messages.

5. **Flesh out the introduction, body and summary** (see the Plan and Prepare Tab).

6. **Prepare for questions.** Anticipate all of the nasty things which could be asked, and don't take it personally when they come up.

7. **Keep visuals and handouts simple and readable.**

8. **Always do a dry run.**

9. **Arrive at least 30 minutes before** your scheduled appearance. Make sure the Clerk of the committee is aware of your arrival.

10. **Strictly limit the number of technical or subject specialists** accompanying you. You may appear weak or lacking in confidence if you have to have an entourage.

11. **Deliver your opening statement**. You could choose to deliver your opening statement from bullet points or a completely written out text. Depending on your personal comfort zone and capability, either one might be right for you.

12. **If delivering from bullet points:**
    - be familiar enough with the subject that you can flesh out lines in between each bullet point
    - eliminate the "uh" and "um" sound which seem to become more dominant with a point-form text
    - speak slowly and deliberately - with emphasis on key words
    - concentrate - think your way through the bullet points so that your spontaneity can add value (and sparkle) to your opening statement

13. **If delivering from a prepared text:**
    - try not to sound like you're reading
    - take ownership of the feelings and beliefs behind the words
    - scoop read the text - glance down, scoop up 5 or 6 words, look up and deliver them to the committee (for more on scoop reading, see the Delivery Skills Tab)
    - try to follow the 80/20 rule: 80% eye contact with the committee - 20% on your text
    - power your delivery all the way to the end of each sentence - don't trail off because of a lack of breath
14. **Adapt to changing needs,** situations and committee concerns, without abandoning your entire presentation.
15. **Keep your perspective and... enjoy it!**

Pointers on Performance

1. Usually address the member who asks a question. However, responding through the chairperson is not only appropriate, but in many committees, it is the normal protocol. Check this with the clerk in advance.
2. Communicate a respectful, sincere tone.
3. Vary your inflection to maintain the committee's interest (if they become bored, they may take their frustrations out on you).
4. Don't rush; take your time.
5. Pause for a drink of water if you feel your mouth or throat getting dry or itchy.
6. Don't go on too long (maximum of 60 seconds per answer); always leave them wanting more, not the other way around.
7. Keep the committee interested - avoid reams of statistics. Instead, relate your information to real world, everyday situations.
8. If the committee hearing is being broadcast, relate to the viewer at home. You will quickly discover that most committee members will be doing the same thing.

Structuring Your Answers

When responding to questions from the committee, visualize your answers strucutred as a "wedge". Think of the 'thin edge of the wedge' to slip into the question. This means:

- get your message out first
- then support or build on each message
- then illustrate your message

Limit each answer to 60 seconds. Don't turn each answer into a full-scale presentation.

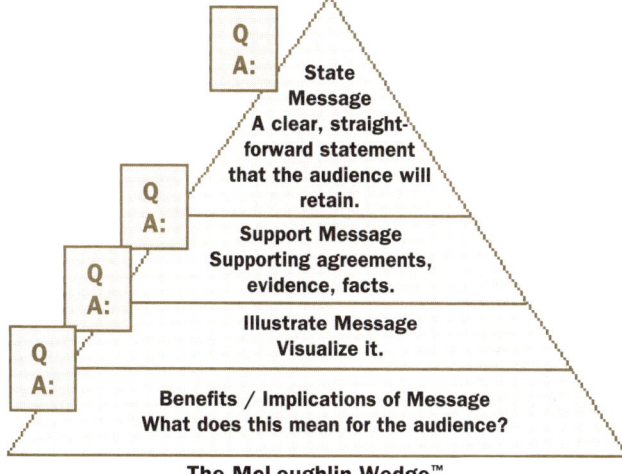

The McLoughlin Wedge™

(See the Encountering the Media® Pocket Tips Booklet for more details.)

Communicate With Power Committee Statement Planner™

Introduction - 10%
Subject: _____
Goal: _____
Outline: _____
Motivation: _____
Theme: _____
Overall Message: _____

Body - 80%
Message 1: _____
  Support/Evidence: _____
  Visuals: _____
  Implications: _____

Message 2: _____
  Support/Evidence: _____
  Visuals: _____
  Implications: _____

Message 3: _____
  Support/Evidence: _____
  Visuals: _____
  Implications: _____

Conclusion - 10%
So What: _____
Repeat Overall Message: _____

Responding to Committee Questions

1. Don't speculate. If invited to do so, avoid the tempta-
   tion. Politely say "That would be speculation and we
   would have to deal with that if it were to occur."
2. Be succinct. It is always better to under-talk your
   answers rather than over-talk them and be cut off.
   Limit your answers to a maximum of 60 seconds.
3. If you don't know - say so! The moment you try to
   fake it, you'll be caught out and it will hurt the rest of
   your testimony. If you have someone else with you
   who signals he or she knows the answer, then refer the
   question. If not, promise to find the answer for the
   committee.
4. Don't use jargon and bureaucratic or technocratic
   language. Keep it simple. If you have to use jargon,
   translate the word the first time you use it.
5. Give strong eye contact to the Member who asked the
   question (but don't turn it into a staring match).
6. Indicate that you have paid attention to issues raised
   previously in Committee testimony and by committee
   members. In that way you communicate that you
   listen to others and you validate Committee members'
   contributions.

Remember...

A bad answer doesn't improve with length. Try to build a
bridge with the Committee, not blow it up.

Media Coverage of Your Committee Appearance

If the media are covering your committee appearance you must be ready for three realities:

1. **The Edited Version:** The edited news clip (7-second sound bite) that ends up on the nightly news or a radio newscast or, your comments may be released as a quote or headline in a newspaper story.
    Therefore, it is important to come in with several 'quotable quotes' already prepared and slide them in to your committee appearance.
2. **The Live Coverage:** Your appearance is covered live on television - thus everything that you say will be seen. You need to practice your delivery as the audience will tend to recall *how* you said something or *how* you seemed, rather than *what* you said. In any case, if the cameras are there, don't blatantly play to them - it will annoy the committee members. Make yourself available to the media afterwards - either for a stand-up, spontaneous comment before journalists on the way out, or in a series of one-on-one interviews. Make sure that you drive your messages in your media encounter as you did in your committee appearance.
3. **Follow-up or Ambush Interviews:** Get your messages across in a consistent manner.

(See the Encountering the Media® Pocket Tips Booklet for full details.)

Organizing Effective Meetings

The most frequent occasion for making
presentations and communicating
ideas is a meeting. Meetings with
employees, Board of Directors, suppliers,
partner organizations, stakeholders and
others present significant opportunities
which should be maximized. However,
the vast majority of time in meetings is
wasted. Think of the productivity gains
if you could organize and conduct a
highly effective meeting...

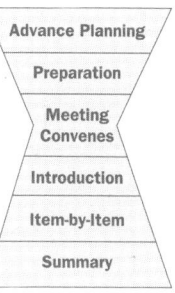

Definition of an Effective Meeting

* achieves goals
* maximizes time
* everyone understands decisions made
* everyone knows what their responsibilities are
* each person contributes appropriately
* a supportive atmosphere is maintained
* a win/win outcome is achieved

90% of your success in a meeting will be based on the proper preparation. One minute of meeting time not spent on unnecessary details can represent the output of ten to thirty minutes of planning and preparation time.

Advance Planning Stage

- Meeting advisory/call for inputs.
- List in no particular order: goals/ideas/raw content.
- Attach priorities to each agenda item (scale of 1 to 10; must, should, would be nice).
- Group the items under headings.
- Re-order agenda with most important issues first.
- Decide on outcome desired at the meeting: decision? discussion only? agreement in principle? identify concerns? for information only?
- State the desired outcome or objective next to the item on the agenda.
- Book the room and facilities.

Preparation Stage

- Decide on participants necessary for each agenda item - perhaps some attendees should only be invited for a portion of the meeting to cover a particular item.
- Allocate time; budgeting according to need.
- Circulate agenda to participants.
- Assign people to do advance work on each item and to lead the meeting on key agenda items.
- Assemble meeting kit including background on each major item for reading/comment with deadline for return.

For a really effective meeting:

1. Understand who's invited - what they need and want to know (a pre-meeting questionnaire can help you discover this information).
2. Set clear objectives.
3. Have an action plan - and follow it during the meeting.
4. Rehearse, plan, and prepare so there will be no surprises.
5. Follow up to ensure that the objectives were fulfilled.

Meeting Convenes

- Start exactly on time.
- Establish the importance of sticking to the agenda.
- Ask for volunteer to act as a timekeeper.
- Move efficiently and briskly through the agenda.
- Ask each person to introduce him or herself (if necessary).
- Ask for volunteer to act as a 'scribe' to capture the essence of decisions on a flip chart or notebook computer.
- Don't play favorites, and don't get bogged down. If you find yourself getting bogged down, suggest that the item be set aside for the end or 'tabled' for another meeting.
- Ask participant who prepared background paper on a specific item to do a 60 second introduction on it.
- As your group becomes more experienced, start to rotate the role of chairperson.
- Try to limit the range and focus of meetings.
- Rather than ranging too widely, schedule another meeting with a specific focus.
- Build in a 5 minute stretch/washroom break at the sixty-minute mark (if, heaven-forbid, it goes longer).

Contributing Ideas at Meetings

- Make each contribution valuable. Don't just speak for the sake of it.
- Build bridges to others by picking up on what they have said, then using it as a jumping-off point for your own contribution.
- Develop consensus around your proposals or contribution.
- Contribute after others, so you can develop a sense of the gaps, principles or issues which should be addressed.
- Your goal should be: Advance the Discussion. Never be seen to be bogging down or repeating what has already been said.
- Keep your contribution to a maximum of 3 minutes. Better to under-talk crisply, than over-talk and have the chairperson cut you off.
- As you speak, hold eye contact with each participant of the meeting for about 5-6 seconds.
- Try ending your contribution with a question or request to encourage a response.
- Avoid 'over-contributing'.
- If one or two people get into an argument, don't take sides. Instead, make sure they focus on the issue, not each other.
- If arguers become repetitive, suggest they get together one-on-one (or with you) and resolve it "off-line".

Conducting Effective Meetings

Tips for meeting leaders to help encourage creativity and make people feel comfortable:

1. Practice Active Listening: listen with full attention, use great eye contact, encouragement and a true desire to fully understand the meaning and feelings behind the words. A leader who listens well encourages better listening among participants.

2. Paraphrase: restate participant contributions to make sure the ideas are understood by everyone in the group before moving on to other comments. This promotes speaker clarity and group understanding.

3. Recognition: Providing positive recognition for individual contributions will emphasize the importance of individuals and their ideas and will help make everyone feel secure. Stroking, a concept from transactional analysis, is useful here. A stroke is a unit of recognition. When people in a group feel they are being positively stroked, they will feel that they, and their ideas, are important. When people feel secure in a group, they are not likely to perceive criticism of their ideas as personal attacks.

4. Differences = Assets: Problems will get solved when various perspectives are brought together - let participants know that differences are valued.

5. Don't Compete with Participants: A leader should avoid dominating the meeting with ideas or suggestions until the group's contributions are finished. Otherwise it discourages creativity and risk-taking. Don't instantly evaluate the worth of each contribution - you can 'cut off the oxygen' of creativity.

6. Don't Manipulate: Avoid making procedural changes, asking questions or controlling responses that support your own point of view.

7. Don't Allow Domination: If one participant seems to dominate group discussions, try avoiding their eye when asking for responses. Or, try a quick acknowledgement of their idea, and move on to someone else.

8. Chart the Progress: Keep everyone in the group up-to-date on the progress. Make notes on a flip chart and indicate when the next step is beginning.

9. High Energy: A leader's interest, alertness and intensity are contagious, so keep the discussion at a lively pace. Ask interesting questions; challenge is productive and healthy.

10. Deal with side-talk among participants politely but firmly. Don't single anyone out, but start by looking in the direction of the key culprits. Then a general request to all to save the side conversations for later..

Creating a Win-Win Atmosphere

As a meeting leader, when you notice negativity is taking hold, you must intervene.

- Suggest a break.
- Speak privately to the most destructive participant.
- Restate discussion guidelines (include not judging ideas, but welcoming them).
- Name the resistance in a non-aggressive tone (verbalize the negativity you are noticing) e.g. "We're getting bogged down in detail." Then be silent and force the contributor to confront his or her own reality.
- Demonstrate a win-win approach in your communications:
  - listen carefully to each comment
  - make notes
  - pick up on previous comments which create feelings of inclusiveness
  - bridge from previous speaker's comments e.g. "I just want to pick up on what Brenda has said..."

- As the leader, try not to dominate the discussion.
- Remain neutral: fact- or opinion-gathering mode will encourage participation and sharing of ideas.
- Encourage silent participants by making eye contact and asking for their thoughts.
- Don't get bogged down in arguments or details.
- Remind participants of the need to focus on the meeting goals.
- Ask open-ended questions to encourage input and ideas.
- Ask closed questions (those which require a 1 or 2-word answer) for clarity and to bring closure to an issue.
- Summarize at the beginning and end. Tell the group succinctly the backdrop to the meeting at the outset; and review decisions and steps at the end.
- Gain consensus on time-frame for the next meeting.

Vocabulary and Skills for Effective Meetings

Move away from...	and towards...
Subjective "I think"	Objective "There are several options..."
Instant Judgment	Delayed Judgment
Value-laden "good/bad"	Non value-laden
Instant Advice-giving	Outlining Alternatives
"If I were you:"	"It's your decision."
Pushing	Letting Decisions Happen
Giving Answers	Asking Questions
"You should (must)..."	"You could consider..."
"*The* way to proceed..."	"*One* way to proceed..."
Emotional	Non-emotional
Talking	Active Listening
Monologue	Dialogue
Taking the Credit	Giving Credit
Surface or Appearance	Underlying Reality
Impatience	Patience
Rigidity	Flexibility
Taking Sole Responsibility	Encouraging Responsibility
Narrow "The trees..."	Big Picture "The forest..."

Thinking Clearly

Problems in clear-thinking sometimes occur due to:
- inattention
- lack of sleep
- emotional disturbance
- rushing or hurried pacing
- not building in pauses before speaking
- not taking time to organize thoughts beforehand

To Improve Your Clarity of Mind...

- listen to what is being said
  - listen for principles being stated, or ignored
  - listen for contradictions in logic or action
  - listen for sequence of what is being proposed
- begin by summarizing what has been stated or agreed
- make a note of these points in logical or sequential order
- add your own notes to these points under organized categories such as:
  - what has been done so far
  - what appears to be missing
  - what needs clarification
  - options or proposed action
  - my understanding of the problem (seek agreement on that understanding)
  - identify the decision(s) that need to be made next
  - give a brief overview of the full picture
  - your observations
  - questions which need to be addressed

Communicating Clearly

- pause before you speak
- build into your presentation some time for your audience to absorb and for you to collect your thoughts
- speak slowly and deliberately
- use fewer words, rather than too many - this will indicate that there may be more depth to explore
- employ an animated face and gestures to convey thoughtfulness and sincerity

How to Gain Consensus Among Competing Views

An interactive "meeting" style works best in which the participants have input at each stage of the meeting.

List the issues, then let the group participate in the remaining steps. Computer-generated brainstorming, flip charts or interactive overhead transparencies would be an ideal aid in developing new ideas.

Allow group members to vent their feelings, but retain control of the situation. If you are not affected, do not say "I know how you must feel". Ask group if they can think of other options. Show compassion, don't be "cold" in your tone.

You could stop for discussion after each stage. Or, you could go all the way though and then open for discussion. Your decision should depend on the group members/ audience.

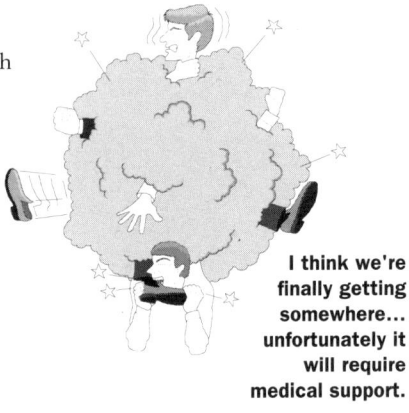

I think we're finally getting somewhere... unfortunately it will require medical support.

Putting a Hold on 'Diminishing'

When individuals or groups in a meeting begin to diminish ideas, problems, contributions or solutions, it can undermine the confidence of others and destroy the energy and work of the group.

Participants can diminish...
- their own contributions;
- the contributions of others;
- the importance of the issue or problem, and
- the capability of solving the problem.

As the meeting leader...
- Identify the type or nature of diminishing which is going on.
- Address the individual who is engaged in the behavior in a low-key, sincere tone.
- Verbalize what you are noticing in a neutral, non-accusatory manner such as: "I think it's important not to diminish what we're trying to achieve." Follow this with silence, then move on.

Negotiating Step-by-Step

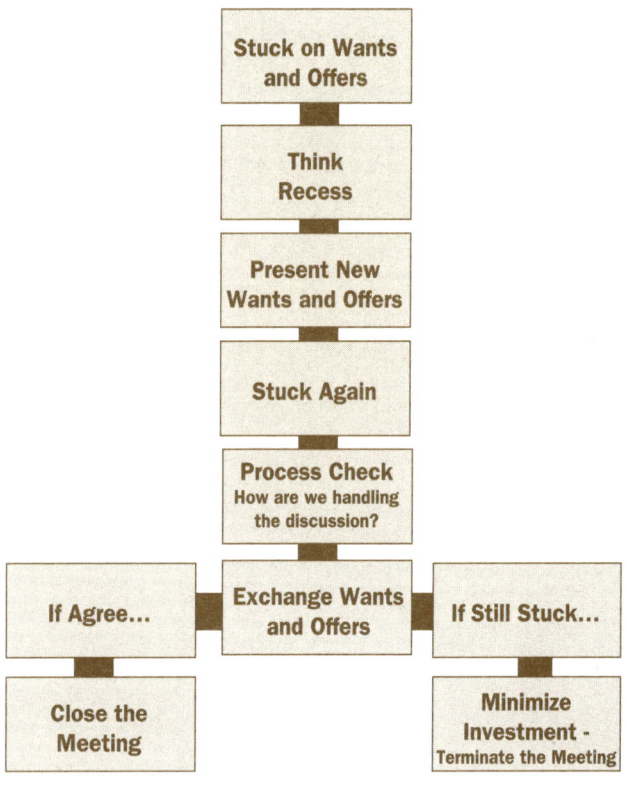

Stuck on Wants and Offers

Think Recess

Present New Wants and Offers

Stuck Again

Process Check
How are we handling the discussion?

If Agree...

Exchange Wants and Offers

If Still Stuck...

Close the Meeting

Minimize Investment - Terminate the Meeting

Steps in Problem Solving

1. Awareness of Problem - felt need
    A (what is)   B (what should be)
2. Diagnosis and Identification - clarification of problem and group consensus about the problem
3. Establish Goals - group consensus on the goals must be achieved
4. Solution Options - each member of group should prepare and present possible solutions
5. Solution Selection - each solution should be tested against the established goals to determine the best option
6. Action Plan - plan the implementation of the selected strategy
7. Implementation - follow-through on the action plan
8. Follow-up - was the solution successful? was the goal achieved?

Answering Questions

- If you are answering questions from the audience, and are using a podium mike, don't move your head off-mike to respond to a question from the side. Instead look towards the side where the person is, but do not move beyond a 45° diagonal angle sideways to the microphone. If you turn your head fully to the side the audience won't be able to hear you.

- If the audience questions are not "miked" then repeat the thrust of the question before answering for the benefit of all.

- Limit your answers to 60 seconds, then ask: "Does that answer your question?"

- Don't bog down with one person - in the interest of all those attending, suggest that you and the questioner get together after or refer the person to someone who can provide more information.

Inviting Questions

Prompting the First Question

- If your audience doesn't ask questions about your presentation, try asking for questions, then pause to allow the audience time to gather the courage to ask the first question. Then ask if anyone is concerned about any point you raised, or if anyone is unclear. Pause again.
- Don't rush; someone will come in with a question. If, however, there are still no questions from the audience, try posing one yourself - such as "I'm often asked about…"
- It is important to get questions in order to have feedback and to fully connect with the audience.
- If you can't get a question, invite someone from one side of the room, rather than put an individual on the spot.

Dos of Handling Questions…

- Receive all questions politely.
- Use warm, introductory phrases.
- Listen actively.
- Make sure you understand the question.
- Ask for clarification if necessary, or restate the question.
- Don't jump in with an answer too soon.
- Keep answers brief, maximum of one minute.
- Ask "does that answer your question?"

Don'ts of Handling Questions...

- Be defensive.
- Assume the questioner is an adversary.
- Show impatience for a question you've covered in your speech - instead, use the question to repeat, emphasize or clarify.
- Shoot from the lip.
- Sound like you're giving the rehearsed "party line".
- Cross your arms while listening or answering.
- Lose your temper.
- Use the 'Royal We' as in "We feel that the best..."

Active Listening

- Demonstrate empathy for the speaker's viewpoint.
- Refrain from evaluating.
- Acknowledge and respond to points/ideas.
- Demonstrate that you are listening with attentive body language (show appropriate emotion - nodding, frowning, smiling, etc., arms not crossed in front, still hands).
- Suspend your own thoughts and feelings.

The Use of Questions in Presentations, Speeches and Meetings

Questions can help you to...

- Develop points from the group.
- Assure yourself that the group understands your presentation.

For effect...
- Ask rhetorical questions, with no answer expected from the audience. Instead, use a question to create interest in your answer. e.g. "What is the role of government?"

To open a dialogue...
- Ask open questions which require an explanation and are impossible to answer in one or two words.

To clarify...
- Ask closed questions which demand specific or one-word answers to help clarify a point.

Dealing with Interruptions

If you try the "I'll get to that later..." approach:
* you may create a negative mood as the questioner waits for an answer; feeling preoccupied, frustrated, "shut off"
* interrupter may insist on an immediate answer

Instead, try "Snippet Answers"

* answer question briefly, then get back to your agenda e.g. "In a nutshell, it was 250 thousand units. And later I'll show exactly how we arrived at that figure."

If your answer is interrupted:

* be polite, but firm
  e.g. "I'd just like to finish this point before I lose the thought."
  or "I'll be right back to you, after I finish answering this question..."
* never let an interruption detour you from making the point

If You *Can't* Answer a Question

* Explain why you can't.
* Offer to answer it in the future, when you can.
* Protect your credibility and follow up.

If You *Don't Know* the Answer

* Say so!
* Never try to bluff.
* Offer to find the answer if no one knows - then make sure you do.

Share the Burden

* Consider passing the question to the audience, if you think someone may be able to answer more effectively or with more specific information.
* Adds a new voice.
* May result in discussion and amplification.

Windbags (a tirade disguised as a question)

* Wait for a pause, then say politely but firmly: "Excuse me, but what is your question?" or humorously: "I hate to sound like a game show host, but could you frame that in the form of a question?"
* That should be enough to force a real question or an admission "I just wanted to make that point".
* Thank the person and move on.

Repeater (the same question asked over and over)

- Make sure you have understood the question correctly.
- Try: "My answer would be the same as before, so we must have a basic disagreement on this point. Let me ask that, for the sake of time, I finish my presentation. Then afterwards, I'll be happy to join you one-on-one so we can explore this topic fully."
- Be ready and willing to continue this discussion, even if your questioner disappears, as often will happen.

Hostile Questions

- Stay objective.
- Concentrate on the factual side of the question.
- If it is really a diatribe, respond with "I appreciate your point of view" and move on.

Questions Regarding Personal Feelings or Public Anger

Listen actively and with empathy. Maintain strong eye contact and support the questioner non-verbally. Frame your response in the following order:

1. Relate to the feelings of the questioner.
2. State your key message.
3. Support it with evidence.
4. Outline next steps or invite further input.

For more examples of difficult questions and how to handle them… see the Encountering the Media® Pocket Tips Booklet.

Handling An Impossible Participant

- Know that you will never convert every audience member to your way of thinking.
- Do not over-invest in no-win situations.

Handling Objections

- Start where the objector is, not 180° away.
- Use words that indicate understanding, caring: "that's understandable", "many people feel that way", etc.
- Move from the objector's position gradually towards the appropriate response.
- Avoid the words: "Yeah, but".
- Listen carefully and respond to both feelings and words.
- Clarify/specify (ask closed questions - require 'yes' or 'no' responses).
- Use the 5 Ws and H questions.

Why don't we just agree to butt heads endlessly?

Don't be such an ass!

Handling Personal Attacks

- Try not to show it bothers you.
- Don't look at the detractor too much; just catch his or her eye in passing (don't appear as if you're "ducking").
- Display contrasting behavior in your own body language, that is, open and relaxed, and in the tone and pace of your response.
- Speak slowly.
- Go for the higher ground; don't try to score points.
- Don't get defensive; don't try to justify yourself.
- Take a deep breath before you respond.
- Stay silent until you're ready.
- Don't counter-attack.

Responses

- Close down the detractor and get back on track "You're entitled to your point of view..."
- Speak in a firm, calm, self-confident and relaxed tone.
- Try speaking your reply with a "knock-it-off" smile.

Resistance

- Don't take resistance personally.
- It helps to identify underlying concerns: control or vulnerability.

Naming the Resistance

Putting a name to the kind of resistance you are facing helps identify the problems and concerns. It also transfers the problem back to the other party, forcing the individual to confront his or her own behavior.

> e.g.
> You: "These questions seem to be making you uncomfortable."
> Resister: "Yes I am uncomfortable..."

Now you can deal with the feelings behind the behavior and thus be able to address the underlying concerns.

Kinds of Resistance	Your Response
Avoiding responsibility	"You don't seem to see yourself as part of the problem."
Flooding with detail	"You are giving me too much detail. Could you describe it in a short statement?"
One-word answers	"One word answers aren't giving me enough. Could you say more?"
Attack	"You don't seem to like me asking these questions. "
Overly Compliant	"I can't tell what your real feelings are about this. You seem agreeable to anything I suggest."
Changing subject	"You keep changing the subject."
Silence	"I don't know how to read your silence."
Press for solutions	"Let's not press for solutions. I'm still trying to clarify the problem..."

Introduction

If you are a political candidate, a representative of a campaign or an organization which is fighting an issue affecting the public, or you are an industry or community spokesperson, you may well find yourself invited to engage in a debate with those who may oppose you.

Strategic Considerations

When You Should Agree to Debate

- when you're the underdog and you want to gain credibility and momentum against a powerful or influential opponent
- when you're in a tight race and every little advantage will help
- when convention and history demands that candidates debate each other
- when you'll look like you're either scared or arrogant if you refuse

When You Should Refuse to Debate

- when your opponents aren't credible and your appearance would only serve to give them profile or credibility
- when your position is unclear or you haven't figured out your message
- when you are going to be hopelessly out-matched and you have very little hope of coming across as credible

Choose the Right Format for You

There are many different formats from which to choose, but the following is a summary of your core options.

1. **Direct Engagement Between Debaters: The "free - for - all"**
    Moderator merely sets the ground rules and only intervenes if the debate bogs down. The debaters can directly engage each other with no holds barred. Requires an assertive orientation, great listening skills, so that the debater can find the weak links in the opponent's chain of argument. The downside is that it is difficult to maintain a logic flow in your own argument and if you are inexperienced in debate you can come up the loser quite readily.
    Variation:
    • audience members allowed to ask questions - either live or pre-taped video questions

2. **Moderator with Panel of Experts or Journalists Asking Questions**
   Moderator governs the ground rules, timing and order of questions and responses.
   The panel of experts or journalists will be far more knowledgeable of your history, and the specifics of your platform. Therefore expect tougher questions, longer preambles (to prove their knowledge and toughness to their audiences, colleagues and peers).
   Variation:
   • audience members may be invited to ask questions - either live or pre-taped.

   Caution: Don't necessarily try to persuade the questioner - especially if it's a journalist or subject expert, who may never be persuaded of your opinion. Instead focus on your target audience sitting at home or sitting in the audience.

3. **Set Speeches - Limited Questions**
   Makes for a lousy program but is the safest option for those who are not comfortable at debating.
   Variation:
   • a rebuttal can be added following each "response" by your opponent and before your next set speech.

4. **Television or Radio Panel**
   Broadcast host controls the debate and invites callers to call in. Make sure your supporters are aware of the debate and that you invite them to call in. Remember, it's not the caller that you're necessarily trying to persuade, it's your target audience at home.

Agreeing on the Length, Number and Timing of Debates

Length

A sixty minute debate is usually necessary to cover any issues in substance. Ninety minutes is suitable if there are several debaters and the issues are wide-ranging.

If you are a weaker debater than your opponents, then shorter is better. Conversely, if you are strong you usually want it a bit longer to ensure that your opponent can't "duck the blows" for long.

The Number of Debates

If you don't want the election or referendum to focus on only one issue, and if you have substantive positions on a range of issues, then a series of debates will work to your advantage. If, conversely, you want the public to focus on only one issue, then a "quick hit", highly focused single debate can serve you well - if you are prepared.

Timing

If you think you might lose the debate then hold it earlier in the campaign so that you have time to recover. If you think you might win then time the debate for its maximum impact - say, within two weeks of the election or referendum.

The Pre-Debate Strategy

Try never to go into a debate with the strong media or public perception that you will win in a walk. You will be setting yourself or your campaign up for a fall. Journalists and columnists heavily focus their coverage on "expectations" instead of the actual content. "Did Candidate X live up to or fall below expectations?" Try to lower expectations of your performance regardless of whether you are a frontrunner or are well behind. Your goal is to manage and then exceed the journalists' and public's expectations of your performance.

The Debate Strategy

Always go into a debate with a strategy and stick to it. You will always be tempted to stray into off-agenda issues or be goaded into positions or statements which are stronger than you had prepared to adopt. Without the beacon of a strategy clearly in your vision, you can easily get lost in the "dark".

Remember even if you are doing well on your opponent's issues, you are already losing. Knowing what issues to get into and what to stay out of is a hallmark of a well-executed strategy.

The Four Elements...

Your debate strategy consists of the following elements:
1) positioning 2) a message 3) a plan and 4) tactics.

1. Positioning

How are you going to position yourself in contrast with
your opponents?
What do you stand for? What do you stand against?
* change vs. 'more of the same'?
* future vs. yesterday?
* new vs. 'tired' or 'old'?
* hope vs. despair?
* solution vs. complaining?
* empowerment vs. hopelessness?
* principle vs. expedience?

In the minds of your target audience are you the agent of
change or will your opponents paint you as the remnant of
the status quo?

2. Message

The overall message must be well thought out, targeted to, and resonating with, your target audience, and straightforward. Your goal is to repeat that core message at every opportunity; bridge over to the message track and deflect away from areas that are off-message. Make sure that your message has resonance with the target voters or publics that you must reach in order to win. (See the Plan and Prepare Tab.)

3. A Plan

Decide who and what organization is going to be the target of your attack. (Frontrunners rarely directly attack their opponents. Instead they tend to focus on attitudes, or threats or opportunities - high road themes; instead of low-road attacks.) Decide who and what organization you are going to support. (Strategically, it rarely makes sense to attack everybody. It makes you look like either a know-it-all or an extremist.) Target the vulnerable areas of your opponent's position. Decide if attacking those vulnerable areas will benefit you. Then determine if you have an effective and persuasive counterpoint. (See the Communicate With Power™ Audience Analyzer in the Plan and Prepare Tab.)

4. Tactics - see also the Delivery Skills Tab

Your tone: (accounts for 38% of the message on television.)
* Angry? (low-key cool anger is always more effective than red-hot anger).
* Outraged? (avoid going 'over the top') Again, coolly target your feelings, and make sure they resonate with your audience).
* Reasonable, knowledgeable, thoughtful - tends to be the most persuasive. It also demonstrates leadership capabilities. (Don't show off your knowledge - nobody likes smug know-it-alls) Make sure you know your facts.
* Respectful - towards your opponents. Disagree without being disagreeable.

Your Non-Verbals (accounts for 55% of your message on television)
* Stand tall, with shoulders back and down.
* Weight should be distributed evenly over the balls of your feet (which should be about a foot apart).
* Rest your hands lightly on the podium; do not 'straight-arm' the podium by tightly gripping the sides.
* Animate your face; smile appropriately and give strong eye contact into the lens of the camera when speaking to the viewer at home.
* When responding to a question from a journalist, moderator or expert panel member, begin your answer by looking at the questioner. Then, if appropriate, turn to your close-up camera for the remainder of your response to the viewer at home.

- Use your hands to emphasize your messages. Don't point your finger (it's rude). Instead, close your hand, place the thumb on top and move your forearm up and down to emphasize your point.
- Avoid quick, jerky movements and shifty eyes or tight, intense body language.
- Overall, try to communicate a relaxed demeanor.

The Defining Moments – Through video taped simulations you will get a clear picture of what you are communicating with your body language at what are known as the defining moments in a debate (which are also sound bite opportunities for the media). Those defining moments include:

- When you are being attacked, don't let your jaw drop open. Look right at your attacker - whether your opponent or questioner. Make a note. Shake your head slightly from side to side as if "more in sadness than in anger".
- When you want to interrupt - only after the person has had a chance to make his or her point. Then do so with non-verbal signals first - until you've caught the attention of the TV director - and only then begin to break in. You will seem less rude and you will be on microphone when you eventually do break in.
- When you are asked a direct question - answer it directly. Then, explain it. Don't do a long circuitous answer. It will be obvious to the audience that you didn't answer the question. That is far more damaging than giving an answer that the questioner might not agree with. (See the McLoughlin Wedge®, in the Media Interview Skills Tab of the Encountering the Media® Pocket Tips Booklet.)

Your Verbals (7% of the messages on television emerge from verbal sources.)

It is important that your voice sound conversational, relaxed and measured in pace. Underscore each word with emphasis to communicate confidence and commitment, and avoid sounding monotone. Practice your vocal exercises so that your pitch has resonance and you articulate your words well.

Don't let your answers meander or become repetitive. Use up to your maximum time allocated for your response - better to go a bit short than to be cut off by the moderator.

The Rebuttal

Listen very carefully for a contradiction or a mis-statement of facts by your opponent. These are often the keys to effective rebuttal. Try to bridge over from your opponent's point to your issue. (See "Bridging" in the Media Interviews Tab of the Encountering the Media® Pocket Tips Booklet.)

Prepare Key Questions

To spring on your opponents. Sometimes the simplest ones work the best. Such as, "Do you know the price of a carton of milk?" (Make sure you know yourself, or don't ask it!) Keep the question short and pointed. e.g. "Did you vote for the tax increase?"

Always know the answer to any question you ask of your opponent. Otherwise, you could be knocked flat by the response. Don't lead with your chin. That is, don't ask a challenging question on an issue in which you are vulnerable.

The Post-Debate Strategy

Always be available for media interviews immediately afterwards and express satisfaction that you achieved your goals. Be magnanimous with comments on your opponents. Never declare victory for yourself (leave that for your "spin doctors"). Your message is that it's up to the audience (voters) to decide who won, but that you feel good about it.

Town Hall Debates

Depending on the sponsor, the audience in a "town hall" setting can be very partisan; already committed and more vocal than the general populace. Your real audience is the viewer, or population at large as represented by the media present, and/or those in the audience who are open to your point of view.

If there is an audience, get your supporters in it, seated near the floor microphones. Your opponents will be doing the same with their supporters.

Keep your answers to a maximum of one minute, except where specifically requested.

If you are not a good debater, a long answer will help limit the number of attacks which can be made on you.

Moderator vs. Panelists

- Single moderator tends to be less aggressive and is reticent about tough follow-up questions.
- A panel of questioners almost ensures tough interrogations.
- A panel tends to be disorienting.
- It can be difficult to develop a rapport with a panel due to the constant changes in questioning tone and interest area.

If the Debate is Broadcast

- Arrive early for lighting checks and to familiarize yourself with the setup.
- Check the backdrop color to ensure your outfit doesn't blend in (i.e. a dark suit against a black background or a light suit against a light background can be disastrous).
- Always have a stand-by outfit with you.
- Check which camera will be your close-up camera (ask the floor director). This will be the camera you will address to speak to the audience.
- Make sure you are not in side profile. You should be at least in 3/4 profile to the audience.
- When addressing your opponent, turn and look directly at him or her, then turn back to the camera to address the viewer. Don't look constantly back and forth between the camera and your opponent - it looks shifty.
- If it is your turn, don't wait for the red light on the camera before you start to speak. The director will see you in the monitor and will call for the appropriate shot.
- Laugh genuinely when something is funny, don't smirk or force a nervous laugh.
- The camera will be on you at times when your opponent may be talking. Use this to advantage by shaking your head from side to side if you disagree, with a "there you go again" look.
- Jot something down on a pad in front of you while others are debating to avoid looking like a spectator.

Ten Final Debating Tips

1. Prepare opening and closing remarks. Write them out and rehearse them (find out if they can be put on a teleprompter®, but keep your text in front of you in case it fails).
2. Role-play questions and answers prior to the debate.
3. Scrutinize the content and tone of each potential response.
4. Work on relaxation exercises.
5. Make sure to have as many supporters as possible welcome you at the door, and in the audience.
6. Have other spokespersons on hand to talk to the media after the debate to reinforce winning points and to deflect weak ones.
7. Focus on the opponent's line of reasoning, rather than on personal attacks in order to win.
8. Hone in on the opponent whose credibility you most need to challenge in order to win.
9. If the candidate is popular, but the leader is not, focus on the leader or the party. Conversely, if the leader is popular, never mention him or her by name, and focus on the candidate or the party.
10. Prepare your messages, positioning statements, and bridges.